AF506271

DEBATING DIALECT

DEBATING DIALECT

Essays on the Philosophy of Dialect Study

Edited by

ROBERT PENHALLURICK

UNIVERSITY OF WALES PRESS

CARDIFF

2000

British Library Cataloguing-in-Publication Data.
A catalogue record for this book is available from the British Library.

ISBN 0–7083–1669–7

Typeset by Aarontype Ltd., Bristol
Printed in Great Britain by Dinefwr Press, Llandybïe

Contents

Preface

This is a collection of essays which re-evaluates dialect and the academic discipline devoted to its study, dialectology. It is designed to stand alongside orthodox introductions to dialectology, and is aimed primarily at students taking courses in dialectology and sociolinguistics, and at specialists in these areas. But given its central concern, dialect, and the fact that the topics discussed also include the history and nature of Standard English, and the national identity of the English, I hope that the book will also be of interest to a more general readership.

As editor of the collection, I am indebted to several people for advice or support or indeed advice and support given generously. My thanks to Rob Bryant, Helen Elton, John Goodby, Ian Gurney, Paul Meara, Hannele Miettinen and M. Wynn Thomas. For her forbearance and support, particular thanks to Caroline Penhallurick. A thank-you also to my fellow contributors, each of whom has helped me more than any editor could reasonably expect. Especial thanks to Adrian Willmott.

Robert Penhallurick

Abbreviations and Symbols

One essay in the present volume, that by Clive Upton (chapter 3), uses a small number of phonetic and phonemic symbols drawn from the International Phonetic Alphabet. The relevant sections of the IPA are reproduced in the charts on p.x (with acknowledgement to the International Phonetic Association, c/o Department of Linguistics, University of Victoria, Victoria, British Columbia, Canada. #http://web.uvic.ca/ling/ipa/handbook).

Also, in the same chapter, a colon following a phonetic symbol indicates that the sound has a long duration, e.g. [ɛː]. Square brackets [ ] indicate phonetic transcription, slanted brackets / / indicate phonemic transcription.

Chapter 1, by Penhallurick and Willmott, includes quotations from Middle English which retain the original spellings. In these quotations, the letter þ 'thorn' is used. Its modern equivalent is -th-.

In addition, the following special abbreviations are used in this book.

PCV   Primary Cardinal Vowel
RP   'Received Pronunciation'
SCV   Secondary Cardinal Vowel

Charts from the International Phonetic Alphabet

CONSONANTS (PULMONIC)

	Bilabial	Labiodental	Dental	Alveolar	Postalveolar	Retroflex	Palatal	Velar	Uvular	Pharyngeal	Glottal
Plosive	p b			t d		ʈ ɖ	c ɟ	k ɡ	q ɢ		ʔ
Nasal	m	ɱ		n		ɳ	ɲ	ŋ	N		
Trill	ʙ			r					ʀ		
Tap or Flap				ɾ		ɽ					
Fricative	ɸ β	f v	θ ð	s z	ʃ ʒ	ʂ ʐ	ç ʝ	x ɣ	χ ʁ	ħ ʕ	h ɦ
Lateral fricative				ɬ ɮ							
Approximant		ʋ		ɹ		ɻ	j	ɰ			
Lateral approximant				l		ɭ	ʎ	ʟ			

Where symbols appear in pairs, the one to the right represents a voiced consonant. Shaded areas denote articulations judged impossible.

VOWELS

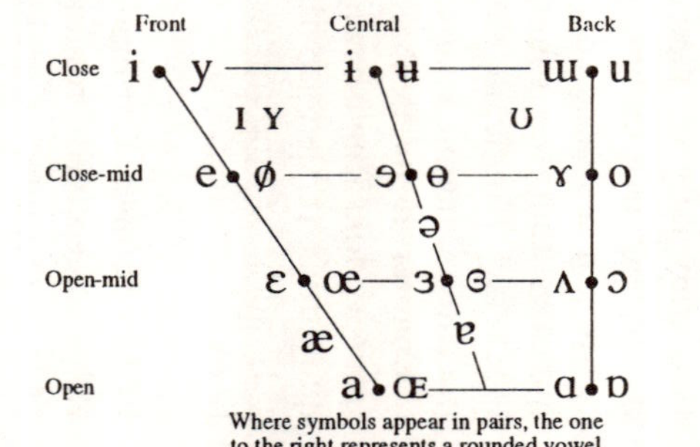

Where symbols appear in pairs, the one to the right represents a rounded vowel.

List of Contributors

Robert Penhallurick is lecturer in English Language at the University of Wales Swansea. He is the author of *The Anglo-Welsh Dialects of North Wales* (Frankfurt am Main: Peter Lang, 1991) and *Gowerland and its Language: A History of the English Speech of the Gower Peninsula, South Wales* (Frankfurt am Main: Peter Lang, 1994), as well as articles on dialect and dialectology. He is the curator of the Archive of Welsh English at the University of Wales Swansea.

Nicholas Royle is professor of English at the University of Sussex. His books include *Telepathy and Literature: Essays on the Reading Mind* (Oxford: Basil Blackwell, 1991) and *After Derrida* (Manchester: Manchester University Press, 1995), and (with Andrew Bennett) *An Introduction to Literature, Criticism and Theory* (Hemel Hempstead: Prentice Hall Europe, 1999). He is joint editor of *The Oxford Literary Review*.

Graham Shorrocks is professor in the Department of English Language and Literature at the Memorial University of Newfoundland, Canada. He specializes in dialectology, and his publications include *A Grammar of the Dialect of the Bolton Area* (two volumes, Frankfurt am Main: Peter Lang, 1998 and 1999) as well as numerous articles on linguistic and literary aspects of British and Canadian English dialects. He is President of the English National Committee of the Atlas Linguarum Europae, a member of the ALE's editorial board, a member of the editorial board of *Idéologies dans le monde anglo-saxon*, and editor of *Regional Language Studies – Newfoundland*.

Clive Upton is lecturer in English Language at the University of Leeds, and a research associate of the National Centre for English Cultural Tradition at the University of Sheffield. He is the co-author of *An Atlas of English Dialects* (with J. D. A. Widdowson; Oxford:

Oxford University Press, 1996), *Word Maps: A Dialect Atlas of England* (with Stewart Sanderson and J. D. A. Widdowson; London: Croom Helm, 1987), and *Survey of English Dialects: The Dictionary and Grammar* (with David Parry and J. D. A. Widdowson; London: Routledge, 1994).

Jeni Williams is lecturer in English at Trinity College, Carmarthen. She is the author of *Interpreting Nightingales: Gender, Class and Histories* (Sheffield: Sheffield Academic Press, 1997), and her most recent articles include work on Dylan Thomas, D. H. Lawrence and Lewis Carroll. She is theatre critic for the *New Welsh Review*.

Adrian Willmott has taught Medieval English Language and Literature at the University of Bristol, the University of Wales Swansea and the University of Wales, Cardiff. His Ph.D. was 'An Edition of Selected Sermons from MS Longleat 4' (University of Bristol). He is a section editor of the *Royal Historical Society British Bibliography*.

Introduction

ROBERT PENHALLURICK

This is a book about fundamental issues in the study of dialect. It examines issues which tend to be taken for granted in those branches of linguistics concerned with regional variation in language. In particular it tackles key precepts in dialectology – one of the oldest branches of modern linguistics – and it refines our understanding of the term *dialect*. It will be of use to students taking courses in dialectology and sociolinguistics, and of interest to specialists in these areas.

The book offers critiques of orthodox views about dialect and dialectology, and as such it is designed to complement standard introductory volumes on dialectology. Dialectologists have always been willing to debate the pros and cons of their varying methodologies, but rarely do they discuss the philosophical underpinnings of their practice. The pioneering English dialectologist, Alexander J. Ellis, stated categorically in 1874 in an address to the Philological Society that word-collectors were not 'philosophic linguists', and it often seems as if dialectologists have taken this as a basic guiding principle. This volume questions in several ways this basic assumption. It offers original perspectives from both inside and outside the discipline of dialectology, that is, from established dialectologists and from scholars who are not dialectologists but who have an interest in the study of language.

The main topics of the essays collected here are as follows: the origins and meaning of Standard English and its relationship with perceptions of dialect; the treatment of dialect in literature; the role of the dialectologist in descriptions of the standard accent of British English, Received Pronunciation; the history of dialectology; correspondences between dialectology and deconstruction; and the principal constructs of dialectology: the object of study and the dialectologist.

There are recurring themes and topics which connect the various contributions. A number – my collaboration with Adrian Willmott, the essays by Jeni Williams and Clive Upton – look at the relationship between regional dialect and Standard English, working with the view that each is defined by the other. Other essays – that by Nicholas Royle, and my closing contribution – also question the understanding of dialect, and language, within dialectology. These two essays also examine what it is to be a dialectologist. Each of these threads is also bound up in Graham Shorrocks's review of the state of the historiography of dialectology.

In the remainder of this opening chapter, I give brief introductory surveys of each essay.

The essay by myself and Adrian Willmott, 'Dialect/"England's Dreaming"', deals with the cultural conditions that led to the development of British Standard English. Perceptions of dialect are entirely tied up with the essential character of Standard English, and our essay reinterprets both dialect and Standard English. It provides an overview of definitions of Standard English and of scholarly opinion on the process of standardization in the history of the English language, and, by means of a careful critique of the engrossing and sometimes startling works of the medieval chronicler, William of Malmesbury, we arrive at a new explanation for the origins of Standard English.

One of the important reference points in the story of the emergence of Standard English is the first use of dialect as a trait of fictional characters, in Chaucer's 'The Reve's Tale', composed at the end of the fourteenth century. Chaucer has one of his pilgrims to Canterbury, the Reeve, tell a tale of two northern students, John and Aleyn, who speak northern English dialect, and who enter and interfere with the home life of the Norfolk miller, Simpkin, and his wife and daughter. Jeni Williams's 'Competing Spaces: Dialectology and the Place of Dialect in Chaucer's "Reve's Tale"' reassesses the significance of the northern speech of the two students. Her main point is that dialect in a literary work cannot be treated simply and straightforwardly as documentary evidence, which is how dialectologists and language historians have treated this first literary use of dialect: as documentary evidence of the emergence of a standard English, against which the students' speech is judged – the contention being that the students are comic because they speak in a northern dialect. This is wrong, argues Williams, and a symptom of

the pervasiveness of modern perceptions of dialect. Williams shows
that literary works are not amenable to such an approach. Her
exemplary reading shows that the use of dialect in 'The Reve's Tale'
is an integral part of the interplay and configuration of *The
Canterbury Tales*, and of Chaucer's examination of social mobility.

Clive Upton's 'Maintaining the Standard' complements the pre-
ceding essays by focusing on the present state of the standard accent
of British English, Received Pronunciation or RP. He surveys the
evolution of RP and its use in modern dictionaries, giving a comprehensive review of its position in British English, and he reminds us
that dialectologists, precisely because they study dialect, are experts
on Standard English and RP. He sees RP as a living, changing form
and argues that one of the jobs of the dialectologist is the upkeep of
formal descriptions of the features of RP, a job which Upton himself
does in the remodelling of RP described in his essay.

Dialectology as a discipline is harder to define than previously,
because it merges into and overlaps other branches of language
study more than it used to, especially sociolinguistics. A broad
working definition of modern dialectology might be that it is the
systematic empirical study of regional variation in language taking
into account the social setting of language in use, but really the
whole of the present volume is concerned with working out what
constitutes dialectology. Graham Shorrocks's essay, 'Purpose,
Theory and Method in English Dialectology: Towards a More
Objective History of the Discipline', does its working out by looking
at how the history of dialectology has been written, particularly how
it was written in the final decades of the twentieth century. During
this period, Shorrocks argues, both dialectology and its historiography suffered a lack of focus owing to the influence of sociolinguistics and generative linguistics. Shorrocks believes that the late
twentieth century was costly for dialectology in terms of data-
collection and history-writing. His essay provides many suggestions
for future avenues of research and is accompanied by a valuable
extensive bibliography. His interest in dialect literature and the use
of dialect *in* literature connects with Jeni Williams's contribution. Shorrocks's essay is itself a comprehensive historical survey
of dialectology.

Nicholas Royle's 'Dialectology and Deconstruction' outlines a
surprising parallel. All of the philosopher Jacques Derrida's work,
says Royle, could be described as 'a kind of dialectology', that is,

'as a preoccupation with the idea of doing justice to different voices'. Royle shows that one crucial voice in dialectology is that of the dialectologist. The dialectologist cannot be a detached, neutral recorder of language habits, and cannot but be caught up in and subject to the effects of dialectology. Recognition of this, and of dialectology's love of the past and awareness of the 'ghostly character' of the present, opens up new possibilities for the discipline – as an exploration of the effects of the 'electronic Derridean epoch' on different voices.

In 'On Dialectology', my final contribution to this volume, I examine two central constructs in the practice of dialectology: the object of dialectology, which I label 'everyday living speech', and the subject of dialectology, that is, the dialectologist, the scholarly observer. Using the words of A. J. Ellis as my starting-point, and those of the sociolinguist William Labov to conclude, I argue that these constructs underpin all the varying aims and methods of dialectology, and of sociolinguistics, for that matter. They have enabled dialectologists to do dialectology. The essay discusses the paradoxes and fundamental tensions that result from these constructs.

The essays collected here advocate new ways of studying dialect, of perceiving dialect and of writing about dialectology (with an emphasis on the English-speaking world, particularly Britain), whilst at the same time putting into practice what they advocate. This book does not do in typical fashion what standard introductions to dialectology do – tell the story of dialectology in sequence from beginnings to now, or summarize one by one the themes or methods of the discipline – though we do talk, sometimes in great detail, of these things. Rather the intention is to provide a forward-looking re-evaluation of dialectology and a much-needed gloss on those standard introductions.

$$1$$

$$\left\{ \begin{array}{l} \textit{Dialect} \\ \textit{'England's dreaming'} \end{array} \right.$$

ROBERT PENHALLURICK AND
ADRIAN WILLMOTT

Prologue

This essay looks at the myth of British 'Standard English'. In saying
'myth', we do not mean to imply that British Standard English has no
material manifestation, but we argue that its concrete form can only
be comprehended by means of an awareness of the racial spirit that
inhabits it. We argue also that its concrete form is not as definite as is
usually supposed, the appearance of definiteness being partly an
effect of the myth. Standard English is a *variety* of English, a variety
which is perceived as being realized in spoken and written usage. The
perception of this variety is shaped by two generalized viewpoints:
that of 'public' opinion, which associates Standard English with
'good' English, and that of 'scholarly' opinion, which claims that it is
the social prestige of Standard English that underlies its 'good-ness'.
Standard English is also an ideal, a concept which establishes the
conditions for the variety. The ideal incorporates a peculiar 'Englishness', a racial spirit. We argue that this Englishness is peculiar
because it signifies a central 'nativeness' which is nevertheless founded on 'foreignness'. We begin by attending to familiar definitions of
the Standard English variety, which leads us into a review of attempts
to locate the historical origins of the variety. We conclude by presenting a different theory of the origins and meaning of 'Standard
English'. Throughout the essay our view is that the meaning of
dialect is bound up with the meaning of 'Standard English'.

I. Working definitions of Standard English

Imagine Britain without 'the Queen's English' or 'BBC English' or,
to use its more bland name, British Standard English. There would

be no 'talking proper', maybe, and maybe no dialects – that is, there would be *only* dialects and therefore no 'dialect' in opposition to the 'standard' or 'normal'. At the least, no confusing or mixing up of 'correctness' with 'standardness', of 'bad language' with dialect. Imagine that.

> Diversity breeds opinion, but it would be wrong to suppose that the images modern speakers use to describe English were equally powerful in the distant past. Most scholars believe that no evaluative distinction among dialects was important before the Norman Conquest, since there was nothing resembling a norm against which variation might be measured. (Bailey 1992, 17)

So maybe, if we can imagine it, there was a state of affairs that existed before 1066, when 'no evaluative distinction among dialects was *important*'. For it seems that such *evaluation* of difference requires a norm, a fixed central zone, and according to conventional scholarly wisdom our norm, Standard English, begins only to emerge during the first half of the fifteenth century.

There is a standard account – or, ironically, a number of variants of a standard account – of the emergence and development of Standard English. Barber (1993, 144), for example, charts the 're-establishment of an English literary language, a standard form of the language which could be regarded as a norm'. This is a 're-establishment' because it accompanied the 're-establishment of English as the language of administration and culture' after the years of the dominance of French following the Norman Conquest, and because Barber identifies a kind of predecessor of the new standard in pre-Norman England, that is, the 'West Saxon literary language' of the Old English period. However,

> the new standard language which arose in the late Middle Ages was not descended from the West Saxon literary language. It was in fact based on the East Midland dialect of Middle English. This was probably due to the importance of the East Midlands in English cultural, economic, and administrative life . . . Above all, an East Midland dialect was the basis of London speech, and London was the seat of government and the cultural centre of the nation, besides being by far the largest city in the country. (Barber 1993, 144)

In such a narrative as this, even though there is no direct line of inheritance from the 'West Saxon literary language' through to the 'new standard language', the natural state of English is as a language that has a standard variety. Whereas Bailey, in his version of the standard account, contrasts a pre-1066 period with a post-1066 period, Barber's version highlights a 1066-to-1400 hiatus. For Barber, and others, it is in this intermission that we find English in freefall, norm-less. Although scholars disagree on the matter of an Old English standard, there is unanimity about the absence of a standard during the Middle English period.

> Until the fifteenth century, written forms of English appeared in a variety of different regional dialects. The consciousness that written usage should conform to the norms of only one particular dialect – that of London and the South-east Midlands – was not well established until after 1500, and then only amongst the best educated and most powerful people . . . In the late sixteenth century, there are signs that the London dialect was becoming more highly valued (in England) in its spoken form also. However, the establishment of 'Received Pronunciation' as a desired standard for people to aim at does not seem to have come about until the rise in importance of the public schools in the nineteenth century. (Cheshire and Milroy 1993, 9–10)

And eventually we have our central norm against which variation might be measured.

That is to say, we fancy that there is a norm, that there is a safe haven in British English, a fixed central location. If it is there, or if we think it is there, it cannot help but govern our view of our language. But what is Standard English?

> A widely used term that resists easy definition but is used as if most educated people nonetheless know precisely what it refers to. Some consider its meaning self-evident: it is both the usage and the ideal of 'good' or 'educated' users of English. A geographical limitation has, however, often been imposed on this definition, such as the usage of educated people in Britain alone, England alone, or southern England alone, or the usage of educated people in North America and Britain generally. Others still find standard English at work throughout the English-speaking world. For some it is a monolith, with more or less strict rules and conventions; for others it is a range of overlapping varieties . . . (McArthur 1992, 982).

McArthur shows further (1992, 982–4) the difficulty in pinning down Standard English. His summary leads us to the following conclusions: there is majority agreement amongst commentators that Standard English is a minority variety, and it is most readily identified in print and in mass-media news broadcasts, and it has a relation with social class and level of education; but nobody knows the proportion of users of Standard English to users of other kinds of English; some commentators see Standard English as a convenient or, on the other hand, inconvenient fiction; nevertheless, there is a consensus that it exists, whether fictionally or not, but it remains difficult to identify the boundary that marks off Standard from non-Standard English, and both boundary and non-Standard English presumably might also be fictional. The document setting out the revised National Curriculum for English in England and Wales (Department for Education and Welsh Office Education Department, January 1995, 3) states that 'spoken standard English is not the same as Received Pronunciation and can be expressed in a variety of accents'. McArthur points out that the use of the term Standard English to apply to grammar, vocabulary, writing and print, but *not* to accent, whilst 'widespread amongst contemporary "liberal" linguists . . . is relatively recent and is not universal', whereas use of the term to include and even to identify an accent (i.e. Received Pronunciation or RP) 'has long been common and continues in use' (McArthur 1992, 983).

It is no good trying to reconcile the contradictions or straighten the zigzags that McArthur's survey throws up. At first, one thinks that one is left with a nebulous working definition of Standard English which does not work because of its incongruities, and which is based on more particular working definitions which don't work because they are incomplete. But any working definition is a temporary explanation awaiting further developments, a definition which by definition does not work, and as it appears that the lines of thought recapped by McArthur reach an end-point, an outcome, we could just as easily call the nebulous working definition an 'un-definition': a deficient conclusion. It provides us with a starting-point from which we can both follow and abandon the trajectory of previous explanations. In this essay we argue that Standard English can be better understood as a ghostly rather than as a material entity. The suggestion of corporeality accompanying the arrival of its name into currency in 1836 (according to the *Oxford English Dictionary*) should not distract us: it has been also a shadowy presence since it got a name and, more importantly, was a shadowy presence for centuries before it got a name.

For the moment, at our starting-point, we are still feeling our way, working with our own vague working definition and we should make one concession immediately. Although we do not want to engage in a detailed discussion of the *variety* Standard English (and such a discussion can be found most conveniently in Görlach 1990), which does not mean that we think the notion of this variety to be irrelevant, we should make it clear that we are not interested in separating out the standard accent or RP from our use of the term Standard English. In our preliminary definition, Standard English is inclusive of standard accent. We should re-emphasize also that we are concerned with Standard English in Britain.

Our next step is to begin to gauge the dialectological position on Standard English.

Dialectology has not totally ignored British Standard English. How could it? The view that 'standard English . . . is just as much a dialect as any other form of English' (Chambers and Trudgill 1998, 3) is orthodoxy in dialectology. Thus, it is, historically, a dialect, social and regional, amongst others, even though many (including 'specialists') often refer to it as a 'standard language'. Dialectologists will contend also that 'it does not make any kind of sense to suppose that any one dialect is in any way linguistically superior to any other' (Chambers and Trudgill 1998, 3). One dialect might, however, have greater social prestige and therefore many other dialects might be judged to be socially inferior, and their native speakers judged to be socially inferior. If dialectologists observe that dialects exist and that Standard English is a dialect, then one would think that dialectologists must observe also that Standard English is usually judged to be conspicuously different from other dialects, to such an extent that it is judged not to be a 'dialect'. Dialectologists might say that this is a lay-person's delusion, but one could argue that in its practice the discipline 'dialectology' has persistently lived up to a name which connives to sustain the delusion: dialectology has overwhelmingly been occupied with non-standard language, a practice which undermines the above-mentioned orthodoxy.

The orthodoxy is undermined then by the very name of the discipline and by a lack in its practice. Dialectology has not directed its attention towards Standard English and it has not been much concerned either to follow through on the view that Standard English is 'just as much a dialect as any other form of English'.

There have been exceptions (some of the writings of the sociolinguist and dialectologist Peter Trudgill spring to mind, such as Trudgill 1975), and we should consider also the impact of views like the dialectological orthodoxy on the National Curriculum for English in England and Wales. The earliest version of this (1990) gave expression to the so-called 'doctrine of appropriateness', described by Norman Fairclough (1992, 36) as the belief that 'different varieties of English, and different languages, are appropriate for different contexts and purposes'. On the face of it, the doctrine harmonizes two discrepant positions. The first of these is that children should be taught to use Standard English, and the second is that non-Standard English has as much validity as Standard English. But the successful implementation of the doctrine depends upon a wobbly assumption, namely that acquiring a new dialect is a process of adding to an old one, rather than a process of replacing, gradually, an old one, or of replacing *and* adding to, perhaps. In addition, the 1990 National Curriculum assumes that acquiring a new dialect of your native language is routinely possible. (And this is not to mention a third assumption, that dialects are discrete entities, an assumption which in fairness it is hard to avoid – the very plural *dialects* encourages it.) And the doctrine is nullified by the marginal contexts and purposes for which the 1990 National Curriculum deems non-standard Englishes to be appropriate.

The document which sets out the revised National Curriculum for English in England and Wales (DfE and WOED 1995) develops the appropriateness doctrine by separating out RP from its delineation of Standard English. This redefinition is in accord with the opinion that learning a new dialect is not precisely akin to learning a new language (that is, not necessarily adding to a repertoire but possibly replacing old with new), and that learning a new accent is conceivably the most problematic aspect of learning a new dialect (it is at the level of pronunciation that 'replacement' is most likely to happen, but also, and contrarily, the learning of a new accent is an aim that usually cannot be comprehensively achieved). Although this redefinition, as we have seen, is a 'relatively recent' standpoint (McArthur 1992, 983) and one which goes against the grain of the general perception, its appearance in the National Curriculum was hailed by Trudgill (1996, 63) as a 'happy result of linguists' argumentation over the years'. Trudgill was responding to a piece

by Stein and Quirk (1995), itself a 'Rejoinder' to another piece by
Trudgill (1995), all in *The European English Messenger*.

> I have over the years done my best, along with large numbers of other
> British linguists, to make the point that Standard English can be
> spoken with any accent, and that it is a serious error to confound the
> two . . . Happily, in this case linguists' efforts have paid off, and it is
> no longer intellectually respectable in British society to be seen to
> discriminate against somebody on the grounds of their accent,
> although of course such discrimination still occurs. (Trudgill 1996, 63)

The goal here is to change attitudes by the strategic placing of a key
(re)definition. But the distinctions that Trudgill makes – differen-
tiating Standard English and RP, distinguishing intellectual
respectability from 'real-world' habits – are indicative of the over-
neat categorizing found in linguistics. The differentiation of
Standard English and RP made by Trudgill and the National
Curriculum is based on the perception of Standard English as a
variety possessing a number of linguistic levels, such as pronunciation, lexis, grammar. Although we have yet to elaborate on our view
in this essay, it is that Standard English is inhabited by a spectre and
that it is the spectre which is the essence of Standard English. The
spectre, via Standard English, inhabits also the identity of the
English-speaker. Such a distinction as that made by Trudgill has no
immediate bearing on the Standard English that we will be seeking
to describe. Similarly, in the arena of historical linguistics (and variants of the standard account of the history of Standard English),
Manfred Görlach's 'The development of Standard Englishes' (1990),
despite its sweeping range (that is, the origins and growth of standard
Englishes throughout the English-speaking world), is of secondary
interest to us. It is highly informative, because of the wealth of
historical linguistic data that it marshals, but its agenda is different
from ours. Ultimately, its view of Standard English is fundamentally
different from ours. We will be characterizing a motivating force in
Standard English – in our present terms, a spectral motivation,
a phrase quite out of keeping with Görlach's perspective.

But we are jumping ahead of ourselves again and we must, for a
short time, remain with orthodox appreciations of Standard English.
In the National Curriculum, Standard English, whether un-redefined
or redefined, has always been absolutely central. According to
English in the National Curriculum (1995), the ability to speak, write

and read Standard English is essential to confident participation in public, cultural and working life (p.2); all pupils must have the opportunity to develop active and passive competence in Standard English (p.2, and elsewhere); effective communication in speech and writing is associated with Standard English (throughout); effective listening is associated with Standard English (throughout). At the same time, the 'richness of dialects and other languages' is acknowledged (p.2); pupils 'should be introduced with appropriate sensitivity to the importance of standard English' (p.5); and throughout the document Standard is given a lower-case *s*. So, we can find liberal gestures which are at odds with the insistence that pupils be equipped with Standard English, which includes their being 'forced to speak an alien dialect – with presumably those who speak Standard English being rewarded for doing so, those who do not being penalised for not doing so' (Trudgill 1996, 64).

Others, like Stein and Quirk, see more merit in the document.

> [I]t . . . protects the child from being falsely discouraged from learning Standard English, trapped instead into a parochialism that would inhibit geographical and occupational mobility. For of course, so far from being redolent of privilege and class-based restriction, a standard language [*sic*] vastly enhances individual liberty by moving towards the ideal of universal empowerment. As a moment's reflection on the Internet revolution would surely confirm. (Stein and Quirk 1995, 63)

These revealing sentiments, themselves so 'redolent of privilege', can be put in the context of a long line of apologies for the implementation of a Standard or a 'best' English (see, for example, Crowley 1991 for a selection, and Crowley 1989 and 1996 for further discussion). Often these apologies have been made in the name of national unification and individual empowerment, this latter cause being a particular favourite amongst some present-day commentators. Others associate a Standard English with 'good behaviour' and require its implementation in order to help remedy degeneration in both language and morals. Those who see less worth in the National Curriculum agree with the notion of empowerment but insist that attempting to implement Standard English does not result in empowerment.

> Experience in the USA and elsewhere suggests very strongly that teaching, in the case of socially symbolic social dialects [*sic*], is not

necessarily accompanied by learning . . . The danger is that establishing spoken Standard English as a desirable norm to aim at will not
only advantage the minority who already speak it when they come
into school, but leave the majority with the strong impression that
their own speech is inferior . . . (Trudgill 1996, 65)

Add to this scenario the difficulty of implementing successfully a
policy which treats the learning of a new dialect as a straightforward
matter (see Fairclough 1992, and Cheshire and Milroy 1993 for
critiques of the policy), and the outcome is more likely to be sharper
exclusion than empowerment. The prestige of Standard English will
have been boosted, and non-Standard speakers will continue to be
ineffective Standard users. The debate rumbles on. More recent
contributions include the excitable (see Honey 1997) and the
reflective (see Bex and Watts 1999). (In the USA in the late 1990s,
essentially the same debate focused around the status of 'Ebonics' or
'African-American Vernacular English' in relation to a standard
English, and in relation to English generally.)

Before we move on to look at history, we should make another
concession. With regard to the variety Standard English and with
regard to usage, we have to distinguish between writing and speech.
In English, there appears to be a symbiotic and influential relationship between *print* and Standard English: the one needs the other
(although a moment's reflection on the Internet revolution might
lead one to wonder whether the bond is slackening as 'printed'
English becomes more conversational). Consequently, run-of-the-
mill written English has come to have no alternative medium to
Standard English. But spoken Standard English, inclusive of RP or
not, has never existed – not if we equate Standard with norm and
norm with normal or common usage, for the native speakers of
Standard English are and have always been a minority in Britain and
the world. Especially if we include the standard accent, Standard
English has never become a norm *in use*. This is, however, deliberately to confuse extent of use with the norm as a model to be aimed
at, but one of the mythic trappings of Standard English is that it is
perceived habitually as normal or common usage. In this essay, we
wish, temporarily, to separate use/usage from the norm as a model,
and the norm as a model from the ghost that inhabits it. Standard
English is now, and was before it had its current name, a norm in
ideal and an ideal of the normal. Our position is that pursuit of an

unequivocal definition of the variety Standard English would be a wild-goose chase. We are interested in the *ideal* of a best English. We are interested in why it is so often appealed to and in the nature of its delusory centrality. We wonder how it came about.

We'll proceed by looking next at the purported origins of the entity that came to be named Standard English.

II. *An arrival-case: Standard Old English*

To summarize in broad terms, it is usually said that the end of the Middle English period is indicated by (amongst other things) the advent of printing in the second half of the fifteenth century and by the emergence of that which came to be known as Standard English, which means that our modern perceptions of British English, of, crucially, a central Standard and deviant dialects, can be traced back thus far. The reasoning is that before the materializing of modern British Standard English everything was different, for there was no norm, and no evaluative discrimination of dialects. Before the end of the Middle English period, the story goes, there were only regional dialects of English, although some commentators (such as Barber 1993) say that, before the Normans, Alfred the Great's West Saxon dialect of Old English became a literary standard.

This is an appealing story, but it is beset with problems. We shall look at the juncture marking the end of Middle English and the beginnings of Standard English shortly, but first we shall examine briefly the postulation of a literary standard in the Old English period.

Barber (1993, 104) says: 'The unification of England under the West Saxon kings [Alfred's successors, by the second half of the tenth century] led to the recognition of the West Saxon dialect as a literary standard.' Recognition by whom? Are we talking here of recognition by (a section of) the tenth-century population, or of recognition by modern-day scholars, or by both groups? Barber's analysis joins two elements in a familiar – to the modern mind – combination: the notion of a unified nation with the notion of a standard variety of its language. The suggestion is not that literary West Saxon is the direct ancestor of modern Standard English, but that literary West Saxon is worthy of the label 'standard', presumably because it is reminiscent of modern Standard English.

Whilst Barber acknowledges that 'The bulk of our records … are in the West Saxon dialect' (1993, 105) and appears aware that the only region in Anglo-Saxon England to escape devastation by the Danes was Wessex, his belief in the Old English (West Saxon) standard is unaffected. He sees it as a corollary of West Saxon political pre-eminence late in the Old English period, after the Viking devastations. Nonetheless, as most Old English survives for us in West Saxon, and as much written in other dialects has been lost, this alone might make West Saxon appear widespread, even 'standard', to the modern eye. Bailey (1992, 19) carries our argument a little way, holding that translators of Latin texts into Old English during Alfred's reign (born 849, died 901) merely 'employed the variety of English most comfortable to them – the kind of English they themselves spoke'. This is to propose an uncomfortably simple correspondence between the written and the spoken. But, setting that aside at this point, to presume that Alfred's West Saxon was the harbinger of standard Old English, Bailey continues, is to presume that that 'standard' was/is like the modern notion of a 'standard language', that is, that it 'is uniform and generally accepted as the norm', whereas 'These translations represent a plurality of written Englishes that were set apart from the even greater diversity of spoken varieties.'

Yet, despite his caution over the use of the term 'standard' to refer to any kind of pre-1066 English, Bailey does go looking for early prestigious varieties. He notes, for example, the possibility that a 'prestige variety', that of the midlands of England, 'arising between AD 700 and 850, influenced the English of serious, formal *written* documents' (1992, 17; Bailey's italics). In the end, this claim is perhaps not so dissimilar to that made for later West Saxon by Barber. In addition, Bailey seems to be arguing that later, tenth-century West Saxon could not be a standard because earlier, ninth-century West Saxon was not a forerunner of a standard. Görlach's (1990) essay, typically meticulous on this matter, is helpful in distinguishing Alfred's West Saxon ('he did not … create a unified written language', p.16) from the 'fairly homogeneous' (p.16) late, written West Saxon of the tenth century. Görlach is careful not to make great claims for this 'fairly homogeneous' *prose* variety, although even he is tempted into slipping from talk of 'homogenization' to mention of 'standardization' (p.16).

Although our summary has become convoluted, it conveys an obvious message. We are thoroughly accustomed to a vision in which English includes/has/needs a standard. It is not necessarily helpful to use the term 'standard' with reference to Old English, or to go seeking standard-like varieties, whether they be regional, social or stylistic. Historians of the language and editors of Old English texts have attempted regularly to locate and specify standard Old Englishes, but as Scragg (1992, lxxi), for example, reminds us, our terms for all kinds of Old English are inexact and 'relate more to scriptorium traditions than to spoken dialects or to geographical areas' or to historical date. All that we can achieve with regard to the correlation between prestige and varieties of spoken and written Old English is speculation. It may well be more fruitful to consider the paradoxical task facing any sort of historian, that is, having to determine the past whilst remaining in the present. The perspective of the modern leads very easily to a rewriting of the present into the past. History-writing is assumed to be a discovery process, revealing the past in order to understand better our present; but history-writing can be understood as a process of transference, relocating into the past what is familiar to us in the present.

Whilst preparing an earlier draft of this part of our essay one of the authors was also awaiting the arrival of guests at his home. Every now and then he would look out of his front window. He saw his guests arrive. Yes, it was them, in the front seats of a bright red Ford – they must have bought a new car. They drove past and parked outside the wrong house. It was their first visit – they must have made a mistake. But no, it was not their mistake – it wasn't them at all. For a while it looked just like them, even though, in fact, it didn't look like them at all.

This odd but unexceptional incident, we have subsequently learned, can be termed a sub-type of 'arrival-case'. Edmund Gurney, Frederic W. H. Myers and Frank Podmore, members of the council of the Society for Psychical Research, in their *Phantasms of the Living* (1886), describe 'transient hallucinations of the sane' (p.xxxi), of which 'arrival-cases' are a category. They say: 'There is definite evidence to show that mere *expectancy* may produce hallucination', as in the instance of 'the delusive impression of seeing or hearing a person whose *arrival* is expected' (p.xxxii; italics in the original). We say that our example belongs to a sub-type because it is a case of mistaken identity as much as it is a 'transient hallucination' – not quite a 'full' hallucination. Gurney, in a later section of *Phantasms of the Living* (pp.515–17), details only cases of vivid auditory or visual 'mirages' which subsequently evaporate.

But the concept of hallucination stimulated by expectancy and resulting in protracted mistaken identity is pertinent. We submit that standard Old English is an example of this kind of 'arrival-case'. It is the result of expectancy. It is quite logical, when attempting to explain the evolution of 'standardization', to look as far back as one can for circumstances that recall modern Standard English. But the process that occurs may be one of turning that which we do not recognize or comprehend into something that we do – transforming the strange into the familiar. It's a process which can be found again in scholars' speculations on the emergence of modern Standard English. It's a tricky problem, for how does one avoid the trap? Perhaps by considering data that do *not* recall modern Standard English in any conventional way.

We have to gloss over much of what could be a long discussion of how a West Saxon literary standard has been identified by scholars. Our conclusion is that there is scant evidence for a standard-like variety in the Old English period and that we should avoid using the term 'standard' in this context. There are one or two more points that we could make. The endemic regional rivalry of Anglo-Saxon England works against any idea that non-Wessex writers would *prefer* West Saxon forms to native dialect forms, though this in itself is insufficient reason to suppose that West Saxon forms were not adopted. But there is no sign of the pressures which are commonly assumed to demand a standard, not for that standard to be recognizable as anything other than a 'transient hallucination of the sane'. There was no print, and no nationwide system of education in English. And we cannot find evidence that, during these early centuries, the Germanic peoples of Britain felt their collective identity to be threatened by linguistic diversity within their own language. The Germanic invaders did come, soon enough, to call themselves English (*Englisc*), and their land *Englaland* ('land of the Angles'), and to use the term *Angel* even when referring specifically to Saxon or Jute. Their language they called *Englisc* – a language spoken in different dialects in different parts of the country, with no indication that any one dialect was held to be more correct or more 'English' than the others. 'English' meant both the sum of the parts (as, vaguely, now) and the individual parts themselves. There was regional rivalry, and difference/diversity in language/dialect, but apparently no 'best' English.

III. *The estimated time of arrival of modern Standard English*

A number of considerations have led scholars to identify the beginnings of modern Standard English. As reported above, Barber (1993, 144) notes 'the re-establishment of English as the language of administration and culture' during the course of the fourteenth century. For most of the Middle English period (broadly, 1100–1450), English was in a subordinate position, with the dominant languages of administration, authority and, to a degree, culture in England being French and Latin. During the Old English period these honours had been shared by Latin and English. Also, in 1476, the printing press arrived. It is reasonable to assume that the approximate coincidence of these two factors – re-establishment and print – created pressures in favour of a uniform standard, which would be initially a written standard. We will return to this point very shortly.

In addition, scholars have identified the beginnings of modern attitudes towards variation in the English language.

There is 'the first example of the use of regional dialect in a literary work' (Blake 1981, 29), or, more precisely, the apparent first 'use of dialect for literary purposes' (Wakelin 1977, 34); this 'at the end of the fourteenth century in a fairly elaborate humorous imitation of an unspecified northern dialect in Chaucer's *Reeve's Tale*' (Wakelin 1977, 34).

It is thus clear that by this time regional variation in speech was not merely a matter for comment but was (or could be) one of the distinguishing marks of a person which could be utilized for literary and dramatic ends. More significantly, Chaucer's imitation dialect suggests that one type of English is best, while other varieties are inferior. Chaucer's Cambridge students from Strother – a place 'Fer in the north, I can nat telle where' – are the first characters in English literature who are comic because they speak a regional, non-Standard, dialect . . . (Wakelin 1977, 34–5)

Dialectologists have expended some energy trying to specify the unspecified northern dialect in 'The Reve's Tale', but other problems stare us in the face here.

What exactly is the difference between 'a matter for comment' and 'one of the distinguishing marks of a person which could be utilized for literary and dramatic ends', and why is the former 'merely'? It might be that here once more is the modern perspective, where the present marks the end-point of a narrative, a conclusion. We read the past a little like the way we read the narrative of an Agatha Christie, looking for suspects, looking for clues, to tell us how we got where we are today. Unlike reading an Agatha Christie, we already know what happens in the end, or think we do, so that clues become deceptively easy to discern, as they are in an episode of *Murder, She Wrote*. It might be that the conclusion determines Wakelin's narrative, in which, first, over some hundreds of years, writers 'merely' noticed that there were different dialects of English, and second, writers began to act modern, making *use* of such observations. A particular requirement of this narrative is that any writer in the second stage could only have begun to act modern because they were aware of earliest Standard English.

Wakelin couples his analysis of dialect in 'The Reve's Tale' with a consideration of

> the shepherd Mak's imitation of southern speech in the Wakefield *Second Shepherds' Play* . . . Mak's assumed southern dialect perhaps implies that a 'yeoman of the king' (which is what Mak is pretending to be) would be expected to speak 'the King's' – i.e. a southern type of – English, and thus that 'southern' equalled 'Standard', a recognized official language. In all this ['Reve's Tale' included], then, we can see the beginnings of a form of spoken Standard English. (Wakelin 1977, 35)

When Mak the sheep-stealer makes his entrance, in his attempted disguise, he tries to speak in southern English, and gets the response:

> Now take out that Southern tooth,
> And set in a turd!
> [That is, 'put a turd in your mouth instead!']
> (From the version in Cawley 1957, 89; lines 215–16)

Wakelin places this passage in the context of a new Standard English. Placing it in the context of north/south regional rivalry allows a different interpretation. Mak's identity – he is a thief – is merged with that of southerners, and the 'turd' is equated with southern speech. To put it into the kind of terms favoured by the text: southerners are shit. Another interpretation is also possible, in which Mak is seen to be acting above his station, and a turd would be more suited to his mouth than southern speech. The question now is whether he is seen to be acting above his station because he is a sheep-stealer or because he is a northerner, or because he is both. The most that we could infer from either reading is that an association is made between southern social superiority and southern speech, or perhaps between southern political power and southern speech. If this is so, we can speculate that at this time southern speech could represent prestige and power, but we cannot claim that it was 'a recognized official language', or that it equalled 'Standard', not yet. If it was *recognized* then it must already have begun. It must have been already established for Chaucer in 'The Reve's Tale' also to be able to construct 'a fairly elaborate humorous imitation of an unspecified northern dialect', an imitation which is, in Wakelin's reading, suspiciously comparable to a use made of dialect in modern cultural media. Yet at the same time Wakelin treats these two texts as indicating the '*beginnings* of a form of spoken Standard English', leaving us with the absurdity of a preliminary spoken Standard English which is at the same time a fully functional Standard English.

When *did* Standard English begin? Baugh and Cable (1993, 187) say 'toward the end of the fourteenth century' a 'written language' emerged 'that in the course of the fifteenth won general recognition and has since become the recognized standard in both speech and writing.' Barber says:

The establishment of a standard language did not take place overnight. In the fourteenth century . . . Chaucer was writing in what was to become the standard language . . . [G]radually the prestige of the London language grew, and in the fifteenth century its influence was increased by the introduction of printing. In the sixteenth century there was wide recognition of the language of the court at Westminster as the 'best' English, but even then it was no disgrace for a gentleman to speak with a regional accent. Nevertheless, the *literary* language had been largely standardized by the end of the fifteenth century . . . (1993, 145)

Within all this, there is a tendency to set up spoken *language*, literary *language* and official written *language* as straightforwardly distinct categories as well as straightforwardly conflatable, and, further, conjoinable (rather like the carriages of a train, with a spoken Standard neatly following a written Standard). Görlach (1990) is more precise. When he talks of 'the newly arising standard of the 15th century' (p.20) he is referring to writing:

> As early as 1450 written evidence had generally become impossible to date or localize, so great had the adoption of London English become. That does not mean to say, however, that the written English of the century thereafter was homogeneous or entirely rule-governed. (p.23)

According to Görlach, 'the printing trade [in England] found the way for a supraregional literary language fairly well paved' (1990, 24). Benedict Anderson, in *Imagined Communities* (1991), argues that the interplay of 'administrative vernaculars' and 'print-capitalism' in late medieval western Europe led to 'mechanically reproduced print-languages capable of dissemination through the market' (p.44). These 'print-languages' (one being 'the King's English', as Anderson calls it) were 'languages-of-power' (p.45), which exhibited greater linguistic uniformity and fixity than had been possible before print. Anderson asserts that the new print-languages facilitated 'the embryo of the nationally imagined community' by connecting large numbers of 'fellow-readers' (p.44).

The variety of written English which paved the way fairly well for the printing trade can be found in its earliest form as the so-called 'Chancery Standard' of the first half of the fifteenth century. It would, most likely, qualify as one of Anderson's 'administrative vernaculars'. Fisher (1977) and Kristensson (1994) discuss Chancery Standard in some detail. Fisher makes the point that, whilst Chancery English might be the *prototype* for modern written English, it is not modern written English or written Standard English. With the decline of French and Latin in England, a form of official written English had to develop, but Chancery writing was under the control of 'a handful of men' (Fisher 1977, 891), and so is more comparable to the practice of a single, though influential, scriptorium than to modern written Standard English. Kristensson is keen to associate the origins of Chancery English with a purported prestigious spoken dialect, but the argument rests in familiar fashion upon a casual separation *and* fusing of speech and writing ('Chancery Standard . . . like all written types . . . was based on a spoken variety', p.103), and upon the unmindful transferral of a modern perspective ('Being used by the wealthy merchant class, it probably became a prestige dialect', p.107).

To recap, regarding early signs of the variety Standard English: by the end of the fifteenth century there seems to have been an emergent written standard, fashioned especially by official writing and print; a precursor to this written standard can be found from about 1430 onwards in Chancery English. Of an emergent spoken Standard there is still no sign by the end of the fifteenth century.

Wakelin dates 'The Reve's Tale' at 'the end of the fourteenth century' (it was probably written in the late 1380s) and *The Second Shepherds' Play* at 'about the same date or a little later' (1977, 34; though Stevens and Cawley 1994, xxii, are reluctant about its being performed much earlier than 1450). Maybe there is in 'The Reve's Tale' and in the *Second Shepherds' Play* some kind of evaluative distinction of dialects, but surely there is not evaluation against a spoken Standard variety which is nowhere near to being evident, or against a written Standard which is not yet emergent. Such evaluation would be not just redolent of a modern perspective, but simply *modern*. It would require modern attitudes to be already in force, and a modern notion of a Standard to be already accepted, and yet these examples are presented as proof in themselves that something very modern was just beginning to happen.

Chaucer's northern students cannot be comic in the way that Wakelin supposes.

> [I]t is important to ask why Chaucer used [the northern dialect] at all. It has usually been assumed that he did so to poke fun at the undergraduates by emphasizing their provincial background. Although . . . uncomplimentary remarks were made by [John] Trevisa and others about northern speech, to regard its use here as satiric may be a modern way of interpreting the occurrence of dialect speech. (Blake 1981, 28)

Taking this a little further, it may be just conceivable that even to pay undue attention to the students' northern speech is to betray a modern attitude, given how accustomed we have become to writing in, to writing *as* Standard English.

However, Wakelin's logic proceeds in the following manner. The students are comic primarily because they speak a northern dialect. Why is that funny? All non-standard speech is potentially, we could even say intrinsically, funny because it is not Standard: it signifies the parochial, the dim-witted, the peculiar. But was it funny like that in 1380? We can only be certain it was if there was already such a Standard in force. What is the evidence that there was? The fact that the students are comic. And so on. (See Jeni Williams's essay in the present volume for further discussion of 'The Reve's Tale'.)

If we search for the beginnings of the variety Standard English, the period from the late fourteenth century to the late fifteenth century shows us a gradually emerging incipient *written* Standard. We are encouraged to look forward to greater written standardization and to the possibility of a subsequent spoken Standard. If we search for the beginnings of modern discriminative attitudes towards variation in English, we find no firm evidence of anything definitely modern. Nevertheless, the material that we have found does lead us to the essence of modern Standard English. Curiously, given that it provided no clear evidence of any beginnings, it leads us further backwards chronologically.

IV. John of Trevisa, in 1387, on northern speech

Wakelin (1977, 34–5) refers to 'The Reve's Tale', to the *Second Shepherds' Play* and to John of Trevisa's 1387 translation and elaboration of the *Polychronicon*, a history of the world up to 1352 written in Latin by Ralph/Ranulph Higden, a Benedictine monk in the abbey of St Werburg, Chester. Several sections from a passage at the end of the penultimate chapter (on the languages of Britain) of book I of Trevisa's translation have seemed significant to scholars. Barber (1993, 142–3) notes Higden's comments on the corruption of the English language owing to the influence of Danes and Normans, and the comments which follow by Higden and Trevisa on the use and teaching of French in England in the fourteenth century (see also Baugh and Cable 1993, 146–7). Higden and Trevisa then discuss the diversity, or lack of it, of French and English (see also Bailey 1992, 24), before reporting that men of the east and men of the west of England 'acordeþ more in sownynge ["pronunciation"] of speche' than do northern men and southern men, and that

therefore men of Mercia or 'myddel Engelond' understand better
both the northern and the southern 'side langages' than northerners
and southerners understand each other. This section demonstrates,
according to Baugh and Cable (1993, 187–8), how the East Midland
dialect of Middle English was favourably positioned to influence
the make-up of the new Standard English as it surfaced. It does
undoubtedly denote a north/south divide in England. This is evi-
denced further as Trevisa continues:

> Al þe longage of þe Norþhumbres, and specialliche at York, is so
> scharp, slitting ['piercing, shrill'], and frotynge ['strident' or 'harsh']
> and vnschape ['unshaped, ill-formed'], þat we souþerne men may þat
> longage vnneþe ['hardly'] vnderstonde. (From Churchill Babington's
> edition of Higden/Trevisa, 1869, II: 163; also quoted by Bailey
> 1992, 24, and Wakelin 1977, 34)

Bailey (1992, 24) points out that Trevisa's 'scharp, slitting, and
frotynge and vnschape' amplifies the lonely *stridet* of Higden.
Wakelin (1977, 34) suggests that this sentence 'perhaps gains in force
from the Gloucestershire dialect in which Trevisa's translation is
couched'. Why should it? Unless, say, one considers written
Gloucestershire dialect to be somehow abnormal. And do we ever
perceive a written text to be 'couched' in Standard English?

Trevisa, although a native of Cornwall, resided chiefly in
Gloucestershire. W. W. Skeat, in his *English Dialects* (1911),
writes that Trevisa's translation 'is all in the Southern dialect,
originally that of Gloucestershire' (p.54) and that he (Skeat) was not
aware of 'any important work in the Southern dialect' (p.55) more
recent than the translations of Trevisa.

Trevisa's text continues with an explanation of the offensive and
difficult nature of northern speech:

> I trowe ['believe'] þat þat is bycause þat þey beeþ nyh to straunge
> ['foreign'] men and naciouns þat spekeþ strongliche ['strangely'], and
> also bycause þat þe kynges of Engelond woneþ ['dwell, abide'] alwey
> fer from þat cuntrey; for þey beeþ more i-torned to þe souþ con-
> tray, and Yif þey gooþ to þe norþ contray þey gooþ wiþ greet help
> and strengþ. Þe cause why þey beeþ more in þe souþ contrey þan
> in þe norþ, is for hit may be better corne londe, more peple, more
> noble citees, and more profitable hauenes ['havens']. (Babington
> 1869, II: 163)

Bailey (1992, 25) states that, at the time that the *Polychronicon* was written and translated, 'Northern English struck southerners as an outlandish, frontier variety.' He notes the above passage. In their characterization of the north (that is, north as in north of the Humber), Higden and Trevisa associate alien influence, distance from the court and the more civilized south, and an element of danger (from which a visiting king of England would need strong protection).

Whatever the birthplace or domicile of either Higden or Trevisa, the text here is written from a southern perspective. Trevisa's translation is in southern English; he says 'we souþerne men'. Whereas Higden and Trevisa's description of the middle position of Mercian speech is apparently neutral and written from a generally exterior viewpoint, the description of the north is from a viewpoint that is exterior to the north only. From this viewpoint, northerners and their speech are *unfamiliar*: their speech is ugly and strange, corrupted through contact with alien peoples and through lack of contact with southern culture. These characteristics might be interdependent. It does appear that this amounts to an evaluative distinction of regional speech, in which northern speech is compared unfavourably with southern. This does not show that a Standard English was emerging at the end of the fourteenth century, unless 'Standard' relates to a southern English viewpoint which matches the speech of the south with 'familiar' or even 'normal' and the speech of the north with 'strange'. If northern English and northerners were outlandish, then they were being distanced, by southerners, from a centre positioned in the south. This might be a centre of national power and authority; it might be a centre whose language/dialect/speech represents 'normality' – for southerners. In this we *might* recognize a certain language-norm concept, that is, an awareness amongst southerners that their own speech is usual and that northern speech is unusual. We might glimpse also an awareness amongst northerners that southerners believe their southern speech to be superior – at least, according to the limited evidence of the *Second Shepherds' Play*. We have to be wary always of manœuvring a modern state of affairs into the past, but, in postulating this centre of normality, we are suggesting both that the whole of the south could be treated as normal in opposition to a strange elsewhere, and that there *could be* a particular centre within the south that might be normal in opposition to the rather strange

of, say, Trevisa's Gloucestershire. We are proposing that southerners and northerners alike might subscribe to a view of the English
language conditioned by such an imaginary centre – imaginary in
that it is *thought up, thought up* from a particular perspective.

However, this language-norm concept does not amount to Standard English as (un)defined in most modern accounts. To say that
late fourteenth-century ' "southern" equalled "Standard" ' (Wakelin
1977, 35) *is* to transport the mythical trappings of a fully functional
Standard English back into its prehistory. We do not deny a
connection. We are even arguing that its prehistory leads us to the
essence of Standard English. We are not in accord with Leith (1983),
for example, who says guardedly: 'Trevisa could rail at the . . .
speech of the York area . . . differences in dialect were only differences, even if regrettable' (41–2). We are saying that to transport the
modern attitudes associated with a fully functional Standard English
back into its prehistory is to obscure, to conceal the route to its
essence. We cannot talk of a Standard English at the end of the fourteenth century. There was no model of 'correct' or 'proper' usage
(spoken or written), and no mass medium for its promulgation.
Nevertheless, the awareness which we mention above – a mock-up
being thought, by the English, of the English language and its
users – takes us nearer to what we have so far described as both
ghost and essence.

If Higden/Trevisa's observations shed light on the situation at the
end of the fourteenth century, as Bailey (1992, 24–5), Crystal
(1995, 55) and Leith (1983, 41–2) report that they do, then they shed
light also on the situation at the start of the twelfth century.

V. William of Malmesbury, in 1125, on northern speech

Higden and Trevisa acknowledge William of Malmesbury's *De
Gestis Pontificum Anglorum* (= *Deeds of the English Pontiffs, c.* 1125)
as the source of their remarks. Bailey almost acknowledges Higden's
and Trevisa's debt to William: 'Just how unintelligible northern
English was to southerners like Trevisa is a matter of dispute,
although complaints about the speech of Yorkshire had been a
commonplace since they had first been articulated by William of
Malmesbury about 1125' (Bailey 1992, 24). Wakelin is more specific:

'The [Trevisa] passage derives ultimately, however, from the prologue of William of Malmesbury's *Gesta Pontificum Anglorum* (*c.* 1125), and is thus evidence of linguistic conditions some 250 years previous to Trevisa' (1977, 34). It is evidence of a certain opinion about linguistic variation rather than of 'linguistic conditions'. In Wakelin's analysis, the passage is an example of 'mere comment' on regional variation in speech, and not of the more active 'literary utilization' of such variation.

Higden/Trevisa are closer to replicating William of Malmesbury's comments than deriving from them. Here is our translation of William's Latin original:

Now the whole language of the Northumbrians, and most particularly at York, is so uncouth [or 'unnatural/disordered'; the Latin is *inconditum*] and strident [or 'harsh/grating/creaking/whistling'; Latin *stridet*], that we southerners can understand none of it. This comes about because of their proximity to barbarous [or 'foreign'; *barbararum*] peoples, and because of their remoteness from the kings, who were once English but are now Norman, whom we know to be more inclined to the south than to the north. When in these parts, the king is content with his household troops, but when he goes to those parts of his kingdom, he does not go without a great number of reinforcements. (Translation of William of Malmesbury, *De Gestis Pontificum Anglorum* (*Deeds of the English Pontiffs*), Prologue to book III, 1125, edited from the autograph manuscript by N. E. S. A. Hamilton 1870, 209)

There are two differences to note between Malmesbury and Higden/Trevisa: the final sentence of Higden/Trevisa ('better corn londe, more peple' etc.) is theirs alone; and William points out in 1125 that the kings of England are now Norman, while Higden/Trevisa do not, naturally. The prolonged northern military resistance to the Normans helps explain the original reference to the king's need for great strength of reinforcements when in those parts. In William, there then follows a narrative about a strange event at York during the eighth century, when it rained blood from a cloudless sky during Lent, which, he says, was taken to portend calamity from the north. This calamity, according to William, turned out to be the devastation visited on the north of England by first the Danes and then the Normans (who were originally 'northmen'). The calamity was due to the violence and wickedness of the north – whether this be the north of England or the north to the north of England is unclear.

Despite the 1125 original, language scholars discuss Higden/Trevisa, not William. William's Latin original is over 250 years before Trevisa's English copy and the time alleged to mark the earliest signs of 'a form of spoken Standard English' (Wakelin 1977, 35). William's Latin original cannot be used in the way that 'The Reve's Tale' and *The Second Shepherds' Play* are used by, for example, Wakelin – although we have argued that neither can 'The Reve's Tale' and *The Second Shepherds' Play* be used in the way that they have been used. Focusing on this section of William's text allows us only to reiterate our explication of Trevisa. Southerners are within, northerners are without. There is a separation, a divide, between north and south, which is being articulated from a southern viewpoint, and we suggest again that its expression is allied with a notion of normality, a normality associated with the south. If we put this passage in the wider context of our knowledge of William, his writings, his position and of the religious politics of his time, then we have to qualify our phrase 'notion of normality'. We are saying that it is possible to recognize a notion of normality that is connected in the long run with the modern notion of normality associated with the concept *Standard English*, but we do not wish to imply that these two notions are identical or perhaps even similar. The passage evinces primarily a north/south divide. That the Norman conquerors prefer the south is significant. It centres the south. That York was the centre of the old Danish kingdom of the north is also significant. In addition, the sees of York and Canterbury were engaged in a power struggle for pride of place in the Christian hierarchy of the country. Both factors help to explain why York is singled out above other areas of the old Danelaw. The apparent focus of the passage – condemnation of northern speech in comparison with southern – is therefore a symbol of deep-seated anxieties and rivalries.

In the following section we place the passage specifically in the context of other material from William. The religious background to William's texts is relevant to our argument, which is that in William we see the expression of a fear of difference, or, more accurately, a fear of foreignness which is inseparable from an awareness of foreignness at the core of Englishness.

VI. William of Malmesbury, in 1125, on foreigners and natives

Of William of Malmesbury's works, it is the *Gesta Regum Anglorum* (= *Deeds of the English Kings*, 1125) which has provided us with most material.

William was born apparently *circa* 1095 and not far from Malmesbury in Wiltshire. He tells us that he was of mixed parentage, and that his father, who is likely to have been the Norman partner, ensured that he had some education (presumably via a private tutor or local grammar school) before his entry into the cloister of Malmesbury at an early age . . .

The first precisely fixed point in William's biography is the completion of the first edition of his *Gesta Regum Anglorum*, in 1125. This enormous work, on which much of his modern reputation rests, was designed to cover the secular history of England from Bede's time [early eighth century] until his own; in the *Gesta Pontificum* [also *c.* 1125] he would do the same for English religious history. (Thomson 1987, 2–3)

Thomson states also that William 'was a detached scholar who does not often give himself away by offering opinions other than those conventional within a Benedictine community of the time' (1987, 3). Amongst the opinions offered, or viewpoints represented, in the *Gesta Regum*, there is much that seems connected with what Thomson describes as the 'confrontation and eventual osmosis of imported [Norman] and revived native culture' (1987, 1). William's mixed Norman/English bloodline may be relevant also.

In the following discussion, we quote William frequently and so, for ease of reference, each separate quotation is given a number between rounded brackets; all the quotations in English are from the translation of the *Gesta Regum* produced by J. A. Giles (1895 [1866]); references to the original Latin are to *De Gestis Regum Anglorum*, in *Patrologia Latina*, 179, edited by J.-P. Migne (1855), columns 959–1392.

We concentrate on *foreignness*. In the *Gesta Regum*, the category foreigner/stranger/barbarian is used, firstly, to refer to the original native Britons, the Celts.

(1) . . . Worgrez, Lademund and Bregored, whose very names imply British [i.e. Welsh] barbarism [Latin *barbariem*] . . . (Giles, 27)
(2) This city [Exeter] then, which he [Athelstan, 895–940, king of England from 926] had cleansed by purging it of its contaminated race [*contaminatae gentis*, i.e. the Western Britons, or Cornish] . . . (Giles, 134)
(3) . . . that barbarous [or 'foreign'; *barbariem*] country [i.e. Wales] . . . (Giles, 214)

Our interventions in the quotations aim to clarify certain references, and to highlight translations of selected key words or forms in the Latin original. The translations are not necessarily clear-cut. We occasionally add a supplementary gloss to the Giles translation, and we usually supply the original Latin forms of the key items, although the Latin inflexions and the lack of inflexions in English make for approximate correspondences. Amongst our key words there are some which are worthy of brief, general consideration at this point. These are: *Angli*, *gens*, *barbaria/barbaricus/barbarus*, *alienigenus/alienus*. Their glosses cluster mostly around two poles: 'belonging (to us)', and 'being other (than us)'. We have been aided by the *Oxford Latin Dictionary* (Souter et al. 1968).

Angli is used, by William, to refer to the English people(s) as a whole and to the Angles specifically.

The meaning of *gens*, in general usage, could be drawn from a range of possibilities: nation, race, tribe, people; the (geographical) country that a people inhabits; clan, grouping; class or set (of persons); gang, crew, mob. So *gens Anglorum*, for example, could equal either 'the tribe/people of the Angles' or 'the English race'; and *gentilis* 'of one's tribe or race' or 'national'.

The central meaning of *barbaria/barbaricus/barbarus* is 'foreign'. Etymologically, the drift of development was from reference to those who were not Greek or Roman to reference to those who were savage and uncivilized. Our chief interest in these forms lies in the exclusion zone they set up, or the barrier they enact, establishing a within and a without. The possibilities for *barbaria* are: the foreign, uncivilized world or races; a barbarian/foreign people or region; barbarousness, lack of civilization, brutality (can be applied to speech). *Barbaricus*: belonging to the foreign, uncivilized world; of actions, events involving or done by foreigners; rude, savage, outlandish, uncivilized, foreign. *Barbarus*, adjective: of or belonging to a foreign country or region; of or belonging to a foreigner; typical of a foreigner; ignorant, uncivilized, uncouth (can be used of speech or writing); wild, fierce, savage; *barbarus*, noun: a foreigner, barbarian, savage.

The central meaning of *alienigenus/alienus* is also 'foreign' or 'other'. *Alienigenus*: foreign, alien, unfamiliar. *Alienus*: of or belonging to others or strangers; done or made by others, derived from others; unusual, unnatural; foreign, of another country or people; different, other; unrelated; unfriendly, unsympathetic; unworthy (of), unsuitable; foreign to one's nature or customs, incompatible; distasteful, repugnant; harmful, unfavourable, not beneficial; mentally disturbed, frenzied.

There is then a certain amount of play in the translations of the extracts from William.

To return to the quotations, (1) to (3) perform a nice manœuvre, changing the British natives, the Celts, into foreigners and contaminants in their own land. By implication, the Germanic invaders, the English, have become the new native core. It is a manœuvre echoed, for example, in the (disputed) etymology of *Welsh*: 'foreign'.

It seems ridiculous to say that foreigners also are classified as foreign by William, but *foreigner* is never a completely neutral label, designating as it does an outsider.

(4)   Hence his [Edgar's, king 959–75; born 944] fame being noised abroad, foreigners [*alienigenae*], ['continental'] Saxons, Flemings, and even Danes, frequently sailed hither, and were on terms of intimacy with Edgar, though their arrival was highly prejudicial to the natives [*provincialibus*]: for from the Saxons they learned an untameable ferocity of mind; from the Flemings an unmanly delicacy of body; and from the Danes drunkenness; though they were before free from such propensities, and disposed to observe their own customs with native simplicity [*naturali simplicitate*] rather than admire those of others. For this history justly and deservedly blames him . . . (Giles, 148)

Outsiders are always non-members, 'non-belongers', other, embodying strangeness, the unknown and (potential) danger. *Barbarians*, even when the label in its earliest forms signified merely 'foreigners', have always represented the inferior, no doubt because of their strangeness and (potential) danger. In (4), the foreigner is a *foreign body*, a regrettable contaminant in and of an English body that was previously unsullied and natively simple.

We already know, from the Prologue to book III of the *Gesta Pontificum*, that William is able to characterize northern England as tainted because of contact with the foreign, and also because of remoteness from what we therefore assume to be an untainted southern centre. The *Gesta Regum* both recalls and complicates this apparently southern view.

(5) This [remotest] region [bordering Scotland], formerly exhaling the grateful odour of monasteries, or glittering with a multitude of cities built by the Romans, now desolate through the ancient devastations of the Danes, or those more recent of the Normans, presents but little to allure the mind. (Giles, 54)

(6) Of this man [Ida, king of Northumbria 547–59], and of others, in their respective places, I could lineally trace the descent [from Woden], were it not that the very names, of uncouth sound [or 'which barbarous words have a certain stridency'; *ipsa vocabula barbarum quiddam stridentia*], would be less agreeable to my readers than I wish. (Giles, 41)

(5) is part of a passage in which remoteness is accentuated: the birth-place of Bede is described as the 'remotest region' (bordering Scotland) of an already remote land, that is, England, a land 'not thoroughly known by many geographers' (Giles, 54). Here is a doubling of remoteness which unsettlingly informs the apparently southern perspective; the disdain for the (far) north calls to mind the well-known Malmesbury/Higden/Trevisa commentary, but the southern centre is now also in a remote part of the world. And the north, thanks to the Church and the Romans, was formerly civilized, but is now in ruins, thanks to the calamities visited on it by the more recent foreigners, the Danes and the Normans. (6) repeats a distaste for barbarous names (see (1)), with particular reference, it seems, to a king of Northumbria. However, here the names of a certain stridency are those of the descendants of Woden, that is, the kings of Kent, Mercia and Wessex, as well as of Northumbria. It is from 'the celebrated' Woden that 'almost all the royal families of these barbarous nations [or 'foreign tribes', *barbarum gentium*, that is, of Germany – the Angles, Saxons and Jutes, and the Vandals, the Goths, the Lombards, and the Normans] deduce their origin' (Giles, 8). At this point in William, the tribes or nations of the Angles are described as *delirantes*, that is, 'raving' or 'foolish', by reason of dedicating the fourth day of their week to Woden. Thus

the English, southerners included, and the Normans, are put in the barbarous/foreign category – but this is because their ancestors were heathen. Consequently, the Germanic names of their ancestors can be characterized as barbaric by a Christian writing in Latin. In other respects, the Germanic invaders of Britain are worthy of praise, for their courage, for example: 'From Germany, then, there first came into Britain, an inconsiderable number indeed, but well able to make up for their paucity by their courage' (Giles, 8). And we are told that Ida of Northumbria 'reflected much splendour on his illustrious descent, by his pure and unsullied manners' (Giles, 41).

Let's summarize some of what we can infer so far from William's narrative. The north of England, distinguished from the south, has *become* tainted. The 'imagined' centrality of the south rests upon and is a reaction to its remoteness in the (Christian) world. The English are distinguished from certain foreigners and are, it seems, imagined to be civilized or free from impurities in contrast to these foreigners; but we can see that their imagined civilized state rests upon and is a reaction to their own heathen, barbaric ancestry. Their imagined refinement has in recent times been corrupted through contact with foreigners. We can see that their position as natives of Britain disguises their own former foreignness. *Englishness*, depending on the context, belongs to the descendants of the Germanic invaders as a whole, or, more particularly, to a southern core, whose former foreignness has been redeemed, unlike the foreignness of the northern English, which has been renewed.

In William, there are some foreigners whose influence can be beneficial, such as the Romans and the Normans. The attitude to the Normans, however, is notably ambivalent. The Normans too have a northern, Germanic, heathen ancestry, and they are foreign; but they had been settled in the north of France for over 150 years by the time of the devastation of the north of England (by William the Conqueror in 1069) noted in (5), and William of Malmesbury identifies the Franks with civilized ways.

(7a)   And, in order to obtain foreign [*barbara*] connections, he [Ethelbert, ruler of Kent from 560 to 616, and subjugator of most of England] entered into affinity with the king of France, by marrying his daughter Bertha. And now by this connection with the Franks, the nation, hitherto savage and wedded to its own customs, began daily

> to divest itself of its rustic propensities [*silvestres animos*] and incline
> to gentler manners. (Giles, 12)

In comparing this with (4), we see that whereas contact with
Flemings, Danes and continental Saxons is judged to be deleterious
to the 'native simplicity' of the English, contact with the Franks is
healthy, encouraging the English to rid themselves of their 'rustic
propensities'. The passage continues:

(7b)   To this was added the very exemplary life of bishop Luidhard, who
       had come over with the queen, by which, though silently, he allured
       the king to the knowledge of Christ our Lord. Hence it arose, that his
       mind, already softened, easily yielded to the preaching of the blessed
       Augustine; and he was the first of all his race who renounced the
       errors of paganism, that he might obscure, by the glory of his faith,
       those whom he surpassed in power. This, indeed, is spotless nobility;
       this, exalted virtue; to excel in worth those whom you exceed in rank.
       (Giles, 12–13)

(8)   [Sigebert, third king of the East Angles, who died *c.*637, was]
       polished [or 'turned aside'; *nutritura exutus*] from all barbarism
       [*barbariem*] by his education among the Franks. For, being driven
       into banishment . . . and for a long time associating with them, he
       had received the rites of Christianity, which, on his coming into
       power he graciously communicated to the whole of his kingdom, and
       also instituted schools of learning in different places. (Giles, 89)

(9)   Egbert [king of Wessex 802–39, and ruler of all England from 829],
       passing the sea, went into France; a circumstance which I attribute to
       the counsels of God, that a man destined to rule so great a kingdom
       might learn the art of goverment from the Franks [at the court of
       Charlemagne]; for this people has no competitor among all the Western
       nations in military skill or polished manners [or 'courteousness';
       comitate]. This ill-treatment [by Bertric, king of Wessex until 802]
       Egbert used as an incentive to 'rub off the rust of indolence,' to quicken
       the energy of his mind, and to adopt foreign [*alienos*] customs, far
       differing from his native barbarism [*gentilis barbaries*]. (Giles, 95)

We seem here to have the reverse of what we have observed
previously – '*native* barbarism', or more literally 'the barbarism pertaining to one's kin', or even, stretching a point, 'native foreignness',
improved by foreign (Frankish) foreignness. According to William,
the English tribes can be acclaimed for their earlier ethnic innocence,
before pollution by foreign (Danes etc.) contact, but also they can be

castigated for their own past barbaric paganism; and the geographical remoteness of Britain signifies remoteness from the Church. As
we see in (7) to (9), Christianity and the Christian Franks, and
Christian schools in England, can improve the English, who have
been barbaric at least to the extent of having been non-Christian.
Egbert was a particular friend of the Church, having entered into
a 'perpetual alliance' with the see of Canterbury in 838, and William
of Malmesbury's allegiance was to Canterbury. Egbert is praised by
William for his 'uninterrupted course of valour' (Giles, 95) and for
bringing peace to the whole of England after subjugating the Corn-
ish, the Mercians and the Northumbrians. Only a 'piratical band of
Danes' disturbed the kingdom after Egbert was 'possessed of all
Britain' (Giles, 96).

To review further the narrative of our extracts: the Celts and the
Danes appear to be unredeemed foreigners or barbarians or outsiders, and there remains the intimation that the northern English,
whilst being English, are not quite within *Englishness*; but we should
remember also that there was serious rivalry between the sees of
Canterbury and York, and that this must inform William's
references to York – and York had also been the centre of the
Danelaw. It seems that we are told that foreigners are corruptive,
except for some Christian foreigners, who can be credited with
rescuing the English/Germanic tribes from their own barbarousness.
Already, we can perceive a split between north and south, contribu-
ting to and underpinned by a certain constructed Englishness, and we
can perceive a series of doubled identities at the English centre, which
we might represent as follows. Invader/native: Germanic invaders
re-presented as native Britons. Barbarian/innocent: former uncivilized non-Christians who were also untainted by foreign contact.
Pagan/Christian: former uncivilized non-Christians redeemed by
contact with the foreign Franks. Foreigner/(ab)original: invaders,
barbarians re-presented as untainted, civilized primary natives. We
can begin to distinguish a central Englishness which depends for its
being and its beginning upon the exclusion of that which is already
its prime feature: foreignness.

We can now add to this mixture William's account of the English
state following the Norman Conquest.

(10) At that time too [mid-eleventh century], on the confines of Brittany
      and Normandy, a prodigy [*portentum*] was seen in one, or more

properly speaking, in two women: there were two heads, four arms, and every other part twofold to the navel; beneath, were two legs, two feet, and all other parts single. While one was laughing, eating, or speaking, the other would cry, fast, or remain silent: though both mouths ate, yet the excrement was discharged by only one passage. At last, one dying, the other survived, and the living carried about the dead, for the space of three years, till she died also, through the fatigue of the weight, and the stench of the dead carcass. Many were of opinion, and some even have written, that these women represented England and Normandy, which, though separated by position, are yet united under one master. Whatever wealth these countries greedily absorb, flows into one common receptacle [*lacuna*], which is either the covetousness of princes, or the ferocity of surrounding nations. England, yet vigorous, supports with her wealth Normandy now dead and almost decayed, until she herself perhaps shall fall through the violence of spoilers. Happy, if she shall ever again breathe that liberty, the mere shadow of which she has long pursued! She now mourns, borne down with calamity, and oppressed with exactions; the causes of which misery I shall relate, after I have despatched some things pertaining to my subject. For since I have hitherto recorded the civil and military transactions of the kings of England, I may be allowed to expatiate somewhat on the sanctity of certain of them; and at the same time to contemplate what splendour of divine love beamed on this people, from the first dawning of their faith: since I believe you can nowhere find the bodies of so many saints entire after death, typifying the state of final incorruption. I imagine this to have taken place by God's agency, in order that a nation, situated, as it were, almost out of the world, should more confidently embrace the hope of resurrection from the contemplation of the incorruption of the saints. (Giles, 235–6)

William of Malmesbury is English and Norman. In extract (10), England is English but joined with Normandy – two realms incorporated into a single state. The English state has a double identity. One is also two. Two who are one, both plural and singular, foreign to each other, yet one and the same. Two foreign bodies making a singular body. A double identity founded on foreignness. One laughs while the other cries, yet one and the other inhabit the same body. But the perspective from which we view this union is English. It is the plight of England that is lamented. One dies but the remaining one carries the dead-weight, and still the dead twin determines the remaining.

(11) [F]or England is become the residence of foreigners [*exterorum*], and
the property of strangers [*alienigenarum*]: at the present time, there is
no Englishman, either earl, bishop, or abbat [*sic*]; strangers [*advenae*]
all, they prey upon the riches and vitals of England; nor is there any
hope of a termination to this misery. (Giles, 253)

This separation of English and foreign, which tries to negate the
union of foreign with English, builds upon an original foreignness in
English, the original exteriority of the English, their original
condition as invaders. The manœuvre which turns the Celts into
foreigners, which names them foreigners, betrays an awareness of
the original foreignness of the English and of the vulnerability that
comes with foreignness, and of the need to disguise one's own
foreignness. This is not *William*'s manœuvre in particular, but a
device which contributes to the process by means of which a culture
of Englishness is able to define itself. Foreigners can be absorbed, or
they can be excluded. Either way it is a fate to be feared. The
Germanic/English invaders of Britain became newly native, establishing a new core, a centre which had to exclude all (other)
foreigners in order to substantiate, validate and vindicate itself.
It might be that the greatest fear of the successful invading
foreigner – that is, the foreigner who has become invisible but who
retains an idealized *intactness* – is the new and powerful foreigner:
like the Danes, or the Norman French. The Danes, and the north of
England, are kept at bay; the core Englishness locates itself in a
southern English perspective, a perspective in part provoked by the
Viking presence in the north. This English identity needs to keep out
the foreign contagion in all its manifestations – Celts, Danes and
conceivably the tainted northern English – but as for the Norman
foreigners, and the original strangeness in the English, these cannot
be kept out. This foreignness, this contagion is in the body. It is the
(foreign) body.

It is this foreignness, and only this foreignness, which can be
redeemed. It has to be redeemed in order for this centre to be. It per-
petuates itself by presenting itself as normal, the normality. It must
be a normality which is exclusive, which means that it must not be
a normality *in usage*, so to speak. It is a normality which must
stay foreign.

Benedict Anderson (1991, 44) tells us of the body of 'fellow-
readers' which developed following the advent of printing and which

'formed . . . the embryo of the nationally imagined community'. Such a body could not exist in William of Malmesbury's day, but we can particularize, through his writings, an imagined national, English identity. Extract (10) shows us more doubling or splitting of the English identity in the contrasting of remoteness with nearness to God, a contrast which echoes or develops the barbarian/Christian split. Not only are the English descended from barbarian tribes, but they are 'a nation, situated, as it were, almost out of the world'. They have become Christian, but they are at the edges of the world and need particular encouragement and aid from God; hence the large number of English saints 'entire after death, typifying the state of final incorruption'.

William's attitude towards the new foreigners in England, the Normans, is, as we have said before, one of ambivalence. The ambivalence is apparent in extracts (12) to (14), from a long passage which follows upon Malmesbury's account of the Battle of Hastings, and which is a digression on the customs of the English and the character of the Normans. It is a passage which supports much that we have already inferred.

(12)   This was a fatal day to England [i.e. the defeat at Hastings], a melancholy havoc of our dear country, through its change of masters. For it had long since adopted the manners of the Angles, which had been various according to the times: for in the first years of their arrival, they were barbarians [*barbarico*] in their look and manners, warlike in their usages, heathens in their rites; but after embracing the faith of Christ, by degrees, and in process of time, from the peace they enjoyed, regarding arms only in a secondary light, they gave their whole attention to religion. (Giles, 278)

So, the English are a barbarian race saved and civilized by Christianity. William commends those who had responsibility and power in England, and who might have been tempted to abuse their authority. Nevertheless, in time, 'the desire after literature and religion had decayed', and England had become degenerate once more, 'for several years before the arrival of the Normans' (Giles, 279). Thus England needed deliverance again. The clergy had succumbed to ignorance and indulgence, the nobility had become wanton and neglected their prayers, and amid such irresponsibility the common people were mistreated and exploited.

William says that excessive drinking was a particular and wide-spread distraction amongst the English nobility, whereas the Normans and French 'lived with frugality' in their 'noble and splendid mansions' (Giles, 279).

(13)   The vices attendant on drunkenness, which enervate the human mind, followed; hence it arose that engaging William [the Conqueror], more with rashness, and precipitate fury, than military skill, they doomed themselves, and their country to slavery, by one, and that an easy, victory. (Giles, 279)

The English, therefore, were not only in need of deliverance, but, because of their degeneracy, they were in no fit state to resist deliverance or conquest, especially when their new masters were so virtuous – though Malmesbury acknowledges that there remained many blameless clergy and laity in England.

And, in his account, the Normans, whilst being good Christians, are also a pragmatic people. According to William, the Normans are a martial race who are also ready to use bribery where military strength fails; they are frugal but envious and ambitious; they defend their subjects against others but misuse them themselves; and 'they are faithful to their lords, though a slight offence renders them perfidious' (Giles, 280), being prepared to use treachery whenever it is likely to prove successful.

(14)   They are, however, the kindest of nations, and they esteem strangers [*advenas*] worthy of equal honour with themselves. They also intermarry with their vassals. They revived, by their arrival, the observances of religion, which were everywhere grown lifeless in England. (Giles, 280)

Maybe his description of the Normans is slyly humorous, maybe it is tremendously tongue-in-cheek, maybe it is either merely ambivalent or contradictory. It is certainly difficult to reconcile the indeterminate impressions of William of Malmesbury that emerge from his writing with the description of him as a 'detached scholar' (Thomson 1987, 3). In the present essay, we suppose that William's writings are neither simply a representation of his viewpoint nor simply a representation of a received or conventional viewpoint. It is less a matter of choosing between the two than of assuming their interdependence and intermingling. Similarly, we do not have to decide whether his texts parrot conventional belief or intervene in the development of conventional belief. We assume that both happen.

William's fluctuating perspective on the Normans reminds us of his split nationality and of England's dual personality. From an English perspective, the Normans are civilized Christian foreigners who are revered and feared. By the time of William's writing the Normans have become joined into England, destabilizing the English perspective. For the imagined, constructed core Englishness that we have identified, the Normans are the realization of a fear and a need. The Normans are the foreign, the contaminant, the successful new invader, the nightmare which will turn core Englishness foreign, even more foreign. They are the Christian deliverers of a decadent England. They are (at) the centre. The centre centres itself by excluding all else. For the centre to centre itself it must be a centre of normality, despite its barefaced foreignness. It can be an exclusive normality because of its barefaced foreignness, which is its guarantee of difference and supremacy. The centre must be different from or foreign to all other, in order for it to exclude all other, in order for it to define and represent a foreign *normality*. With new foreignness at the centre, old England must be presented (by William) as having been in need of deliverance, having lapsed into its primordial barbarian ways.

We can begin to distinguish a redeemed, renewed central Englishness which has a dual identity, for England is now joined in body to a new, ruling foreigner. This Englishness is destroyed and renewed, like slashed-and-burned rain forest. This Englishness which is not English depends for its being upon the excluding of that which is already its prime feature: foreignness – or strangeness or deviancy. This exclusive, central, governing foreignness is expressed in the disruptive, redeeming, renewing exclusive language of the centre.

VII. *The model of a model*

Baugh and Cable (1993, 111–23, 132–53) provide a summary of the comparative positions of French, Latin and English during the centuries following the Norman Conquest. Whilst the spoken language of the mass of the people remained English, for two hundred years after the Conquest French was 'the language of ordinary intercourse among the upper classes in England' (Baugh and Cable 1993, 111). Spoken French was used at the court, and in parliamentary and legal proceedings. In writing, French and Latin were the languages of authority. Latin had become the habitual language for written communication and record, and was the long-established 'native' language of the Church. In time, French became 'the first language in England to dispute the monopoly of Latin in written matter' (Baugh and Cable 1993, 149), in Parliament, the law, commerce and diplomacy (see also Fisher 1977, 878). From 1066 until the second half of the fourteenth century, the language of authority in speech was French; in writing, Latin and French dominated until the early fifteenth century.

Görlach's (1990) account of the history of Standard English is, in its presentation of the general structure of the story, representative of a common opinion. The process of standardization is presented as having begun early in the history of English, in the Old English period, only to be interrupted by the Norman Conquest and the prolonged intrusion of French. In the present essay we have been sceptical about the case for a standard Old English, and we suggest that the story of Standard English begins with French.

The authority of Latin is relevant to our argument, though by the Middle English period its use in England was a thoroughly 'normalized' matter. It is the intrusion of French which is allied to the renewal of foreignness at the centre of England. The native language of the inseparable and determining twin of England was French. The language at the centre of the English state was foreign, used only by the relatively few at the centre, its presence at the centre demarcating the centre. It is barefacedly foreign, guaranteeing the difference of the centre.

The Middle English period has been characterized as an age of great diversity in the history of English, because there was no standard during this time. It has been characterized as an age marked off by its lack of a standard. The standards were foreign: Latin and French. This circumstance is blindingly obvious and its relevance to the development of Standard English has not been completely neglected. Görlach, for example, notes 'the reduction in the functions of French' from the mid-fourteenth century onwards and its relation to the 'beginnings of standardization' (1990, 18). A function for French (or Latin) would have resulted from the requirements of the producers of official documents, and later, potentially, of the producers of printed matter, who desired a stable, delimited written form of language. With the decline of French (and Latin) in favour of English, such a form had to be sought in English (which is not to suggest that a wholly stable, delimited written form was found). Chancery English, mentioned earlier in the present essay, and the object of much scholarly attention, appears to have been the germinal written standard.

But French left behind it another, ghostly void, which has been the object of no scholarly attention. There was a vacancy for an exclusive language of the centre, a language which would demarcate the centre. If it could not be barefacedly foreign the replacement would have to be foreign somehow, in order constantly to renew the foreign normality of the centre. It would have to appear to be used only by the relatively few at the centre. This void is filled by Standard English.

This takes us back to our model of Standard English. The most evident and superficial part of the model is the *variety* Standard English. It is the variety that has been open to repeated, failed attempts at definition and it is the variety which is the object of contestation. Some argue that it is too changeable and therefore cannot be defined or pinned down, others argue that it is remarkably stable for a variety of English. That there are linguistic items, written and spoken, that can be associated with the notion Standard is undeniable. That the number and the identity of these features shift ceaselessly, making a definitive descriptive catalogue unachievable, is also undeniable. The chameleonic fuzziness of the variety is what allows it to seem also to be a *model* of behaviour. Its flexibility is suited to the demands of the role. Its use as the representation of a model is what renders the variety indefinable as a variety. The present essay has focused on the ghost or spirit that inhabits the model. Although our terminology echoes Gilbert Ryle's abusive 'ghost in the machine' refrain (see Ryle 1949), we wish to suggest a thought-up, dreamt-up hallucinatory presence which haunts and determines, rather than to suggest a simple dichotomy of the mysterious and the concrete. We have looked for the essence of Standard English.

It emerges from the ancient inherent foreignness of Englishness, a foreignness which, as the centre of a centred Englishness, turns itself native or *normal*, making all around and outside it seem foreign. Standard English acts out a mythic *normality*. It fosters and nourishes a tangle of myths about correctness, good language and good behaviour, and their opposites. Its foreignness-cum-normality and its normality-versus-strangeness, once recognized, seem to underpin so much reference to the condition of the English language, from perpetual opinion about its degeneracy or its richness to casual mention of an Irish 'lilt' or the 'flat vowels' of a north-Englander or even the warmth and homeliness of a 'Geordie' accent. *Standard English* excludes the majority and, through a familiar twist, places the minority at the centre of normality. It champions the myth of the normal centre and the foreign outside(rs). It continues to express the myth.

Standard English encapsulates a fear of foreignness inseparable from the desire for foreignness at the core of Englishness. With Standard English at the centre, all *dialect* becomes strange. In this way of seeing, in this myth, an Englishness centres itself.

England's dreaming.

Works cited

Anderson, Benedict. 1991. *Imagined Communities: Reflections on the Origin and Spread of Nationalism*. Revised edition. London and New York: Verso.

Babington, Churchill (ed.). 1869. *Polychronicon Ranulphi Higden Monachi Cestrensis; together with the English Translations of John Trevisa and of an Unknown Writer of the Fifteenth Century*. Volume II. London: Longmans, Green, and Co.

Bailey, Richard W. 1992. *Images of English: A Cultural History of the Language*. Cambridge: Cambridge University Press.

Barber, Charles. 1993. *The English Language: A Historical Introduction*. Cambridge: Cambridge University Press.

Baugh, Albert C. and Thomas Cable. 1993. *A History of the English Language*. 4th edition. London: Routledge.

Bex, Tony and Richard J. Watts (eds.). 1999. *Standard English: The Widening Debate*. London: Routledge.

Blake, N. F. 1981. *Non-Standard Language in English Literature*. London: André Deutsch.

Cawley, A. C. (ed.). 1957. *'Everyman' and Medieval Miracle Plays*. 2nd edition. London: J. M. Dent and Sons.

Chambers, J. K. and Peter Trudgill. 1998. *Dialectology*. 2nd edition. Cambridge: Cambridge University Press.

Chaucer, Geoffrey. 'The Reve's Tale'. In A. C. Cawley (ed.), *Canterbury Tales*. London: J. M. Dent and Sons, revised edition 1975.

Cheshire, Jenny and Jim Milroy. 1993. Syntactic variation in non-standard dialects: background issues. In James Milroy and Lesley Milroy (eds.),

Real English: The Grammar of English Dialects in the British Isles, pp.3–33. London: Longman, 1993.

Crowley, Tony. 1989. *The Politics of Discourse: The Standard Language Question in British Cultural Debates*. London: Macmillan.

—— (ed.). 1991. *Proper English? Readings in Language, History and Cultural Identity*. London: Routledge.

——. 1996. *Language in History: Theories and Texts*. London: Routledge.

Crystal, David. 1995. *The Cambridge Encyclopedia of the English Language*. Cambridge: Cambridge University Press.

Department for Education and Welsh Office Education Department. 1995. *English in the National Curriculum*. London: HMSO.

Department of Education and Science and the Welsh Office. 1990. *English in the National Curriculum (No. 2)*. London: HMSO.

Fairclough, Norman. 1992. The appropriacy of 'appropriateness'. In Norman Fairclough (ed.), *Critical Language Awareness*, pp.33–56. London: Longman, 1992.

Fisher, John H. 1977. Chancery and the emergence of Standard written English in the fifteenth century. *Speculum*, LII, 4 (October 1977), 870–99.

Giles, J. A. 1895 [1866]. *William of Malmesbury's Chronicle of the Kings of England*. London: George Bell and Sons. A reprint of the edition published by Bohn's Antiquarian Library in 1866.

Görlach, Manfred. 1990. The development of Standard Englishes. In Manfred Görlach, *Studies in the History of the English Language*, pp.9–64. Heidelberg: Carl Winter, 1990.

Gurney, Edmund, Frederic W. H. Myers, and Frank Podmore. 1886. *Phantasms of the Living*. Volume I. London: Trübner.

Hamilton, N. E. S. A. (ed.). 1870. *Willelmi Malmesbiriensis Monachi: De Gestis Pontificum Anglorum (Deeds of the English Pontiffs)*. Edited from the autograph manuscript. London: Longman, and Trübner; Oxford: Parker; and Cambridge: Macmillan.

Honey, John. 1997. *Language is Power: The Story of Standard English and its Enemies*. London: Faber.

Kristensson, Gillis. 1994. Sociolects in 14th-century London. In Gunnel Melchers and Nils-Lennart Johannesson (eds.), *Nonstandard Varieties of Language*, Papers from the Stockholm Symposium, 11–13 April, 1991 (Acta Universitatis Stockholmiensis, Stockholm Studies in English, LXXXIV), pp.103–10. Stockholm: Almqvist & Wiksell International, 1994.

Leith, Dick. 1983. *A Social History of English*. London: Routledge and Kegan Paul.

McArthur, Tom (ed.). 1992. *The Oxford Companion to the English Language*. Oxford: Oxford University Press.

Malmesbury, William of: *Deeds of the English Kings*, 1125, see Giles 1895, and Migne 1855; *Deeds of the English Pontiffs*, 1125, see Hamilton 1870.

Migne, J.-P. (ed.). 1855. *Willelmi Malmesburiensis Monachi: Opera Omnia*, which includes *De Gestis Regum Anglorum* (*Deeds of the English Kings*), columns 959-1392. *Patrologia Latina*, 179. Paris.

Ryle, Gilbert. 1949. *The Concept of Mind*. London: Hutchinson.

Scragg, D. G. 1992. Introduction to D. G. Scragg (ed.), *The Vercelli Homilies and Related Texts*, pp.xix–lxxxii. EETS Original Series 300. Oxford: Oxford University Press for the Early English Text Society.

Second Shepherds' Play, pp.79–108 in Cawley 1957.

Skeat, Walter W. 1911. *English Dialects from the Eighth Century to the Present Day*. Cambridge: Cambridge University Press.

Souter, A. et al. (eds.). 1968. *Oxford Latin Dictionary*. Oxford: Clarendon Press.

Stein, Gabrielle and Randolph Quirk. 1995. Standard English. *The European English Messenger*, IV, 2 (Autumn 1995), 62–3.

Stevens, Martin and A. C. Cawley. 1994. Introduction to Martin Stevens and A. C. Cawley (eds.), *The Towneley Plays*, pp.xv–xxxvi. Volume I: Introduction and text. EETS Supplementary Series 13. Oxford: Oxford University Press for the Early English Text Society.

Thomson, Rodney. 1987. *William of Malmesbury*. Woodbridge, Suffolk: The Boydell Press.

Trevisa 1387: see Babington 1869.

Trudgill, Peter. 1975. *Accent, Dialect and the School*. London: Edward Arnold.

——. 1995. Dialect and dialects in the new Europe. *The European English Messenger*, IV, 1 (Spring 1995), 44–6.

——. 1996. Standard English and the National Curriculum. *The European English Messenger*, V, 1 (Spring 1996), 63–5.

Wakelin, Martyn F. 1977. *English Dialects: An Introduction*. Revised edition. London: Athlone Press.

2

Competing Spaces: Dialectology and the Place of Dialect in Chaucer's 'Reve's Tale'

JENI WILLIAMS

> John hight that oon, and Aleyn hight that other;
> Of o toun were they born, that highte Strother,
> Fer in the north, I can nat telle where.
>
> ('The Reve's Tale', lines 92–4)[1]

> While we may agree that it is necessary to stand against the dominant ideology of the time, it is the immense difficulty of doing so that must be acknowledged . . . if you do not have an explicit politics – an ideology – then one will certainly have you.   (Patterson 1987, 70)

I. Dialect and narrative

The two northern students in Chaucer's 'Reve's Tale' have the distinction of being the only figures in the whole of *The Canterbury Tales* to be characterized by the use of a recognizable regional dialect. They have attracted attention because of this single attribute, received wisdom for many years being that the use of the dialect is part of the tale's general mockery, intended to draw attention to the clerks' gullibility and lack of sophistication. Understood in this way by literary critics and dialectologists alike, the tale has been cited as 'evidence' of the emergence of a recognized 'Standard English' during the late fourteenth century. Martyn Wakelin explains the reasoning that leads to this view in his bald statement that 'Chaucer's imitation dialect suggests that one type of English is best, while other varieties are inferior. Chaucer's

Cambridge students from Strother . . . are the first characters in English literature who are comic because they speak a regional, non-Standard, dialect' (1977, 34–5). But there are serious problems with this evaluation. It assesses a literary text as if it reflected usage in and attitudes to spoken language directly, as if the question of meaning was unrelated to structure and style. A brief glance at the narrative within which this imitation dialect occurs demonstrates the difficulty of translating it as a mark of provincial foolishness. Though the students are undoubtedly outsiders in the miller's world, they are successful at every level in the plot: defeating a stupid, scheming peasant by resourcefully switching to an alternative goal when the first seems lost (applying the mercantile principles of equivalence and exchange), and achieving dominance in a masculine world through the sexual humiliation of their lower-class rival. Rather than providing dismissive comedy, the use of dialect seems to distinguish two alien figures who enter the miller's limited world and reorder it to their own advantage. The students' characterization by dialect (that is, voice) can no more be divorced from the events and strategies of the tale as a whole than can the tale itself be detached from the interwoven voices that form *The Canterbury Tales*.[2]

This is not a reading that accords with Wakelin's view. Wakelin's comment omits any literary considerations as he invokes the historical narrative of the development of 'Standard English', a narrative quite divorced from the fierce turbulence of medieval social relations. This reductive understanding of the historical and literary contexts involved in the perception of a literary incident as a source of 'information', creates further difficulties when the particular interpenetration of literature and history in *The Canterbury Tales* is taken into account. Patterson (1991, 26) contends that the text is centrally preoccupied with the emergence of different speaking subjects out of the social and ideological disruptions of its contemporary world.[3] He argues for a world in flux, with new social formations and new ideologies emerging out of the fragmentation of older patterns. Any projection backwards of present-day notions onto this period, without at least acknowledging these contexts, must therefore omit a major determinant of meaning. In Wakelin's case, such a projection begins to raise questions about the assumptions involved in dialectology itself.

'The Reve's Tale' presents us with a struggle between two groups: a family defined by their relation to the land and two literate figures defined by their career and their language. The hostility between the two groups is a traditional class conflict. The clerical victory thus implies the victory of a certain class at the expense of another, and the metaphoric victory of speech over the physical world. As a discipline which claims to study language in isolation from ideology, and which understands *place* to be a neutral ground without ideological signification, dialectology expresses the values of a mobile and literate class – those descendants of the secular clergy who achieve victory within the tale. If we look outward from the tale, it seems that dialectology's silences about political and literary elements within its subject eloquently express its covert investment in the ideology and narratives of the dominant class. Conventional readings of 'The Reve's Tale' seem to illustrate Patterson's point that 'if you do not have an explicit politics – an ideology – then one will certainly have you'.

In this essay, I want to focus on the representation of space and place within the tale: elements which the tale degrades by humiliating the figures associated with them – the miller and his two women – and by promoting the attributes of the mobile and literate clerks. This kind of reading of the tale leads outwards to an assessment of the relation of dialectology to the dominant values of our own, present-day society.

The clerks' markedly different discourse proves a resonant metaphor for a class driven by a creed of individual competition and personal advancement.[4] The tale dramatizes the victory of a group defined by their speech as having moved away from their birthplace, a victory dramatized as the virile penetration of and withdrawal from a socially defined space belonging to a restive peasant class. In order to assert the independence and activity of the clerks the peasantry must be demeaned. Told by a figure who, like the clerks, seeks individual advancement within an existing system, and who therefore is hostile to any change in the established order,[5] the narrative is not disinterested but reflects the kind of history known as 'neo-Smithian Marxism', which claims 'the agency of economic and social transformation as the town-based market economy – and . . . stigmatises the country as a regressive brake upon the productive forces' (Patterson 1991, 248).[6] Hindsight reveals the ideological frame of such a history. As Patterson points out, in the context of fourteenth- and fifteenth-century Britain, it is 'the *rural* sector of the economy that is dynamic, and the solvent of feudal relations is neither merchant capital nor the trading activity it finances but a vigorous peasant economy' (Patterson 1991, 252). The long-term effects of such a degradation of space and place to the advantage of a mobile group involved in trade are quite evident today: businessmen are seen as working on neutral territory, providing for the common good, operators who are independent of the existing systems of privilege and superior to those communities into which they are free to move, or which they may leave. These are central tenets of the free market, an ideology constructed through the deliberate silencing of those elements within it which indicate the human cost of 'free' enterprise.

Recognizing the class interest expressed through 'The Reve's Tale' allows the four linked texts that open *The Canterbury Tales* their function as a debate between voices.[7] H. Marshall Leicester considers that 'the tales . . . concentrate not on the way pre-existing people create language but on the way language creates people' (1980, 217),[8] a comment that can be expanded to include *class*. Consideration of the connections between the tales, their reconfigurations of the same scenario (the guardian, the two lovers, the beloved) in a generic shift from romance to *fabliau*, reveals examples of language being grounded in a hierarchal – and unstable – social system. Each voice asserts, attempts to 'naturalize' its own ground and seeks to silence that of its competitors, the struggle being conducted over the issue of the value accorded to the 'natural' world, that is, the space of ground from which the particularized subject speaks. In the first tale, that of the Knight, the natural/sensual world is feared and, placed at the boundary of a civilized community, subjected to rigid controls. The significant boundary in 'The Knight's Tale' lies between a rational, ordered civilization and the chaotic bestiality of the uncontrolled natural world. Love might turn the young knights into beasts – 'wood leoun', 'cruel tygre' ('The Knight's Tale', lines 798, 799) – so social institutions are created to control it: tournament lists formalize rivalry in the human world; marriage rites formalize and license sexual attraction and intercourse, and incorporate them into law. In the second, 'The Miller's Tale', sensual and natural pleasures are celebrated and placed within a concrete human world. This includes the city with its streets, the many-chambered house of the carpenter, and the role of Alison as a figure with legitimate desires. But in the third – which I take to be the deciding tale – the sense of community within which

the previous tales have operated is negated and the sensual, physical
world is translated into a commodity within a system of exchange.
Divisions lie within the human community, which is fractured along
class lines: the boundary is discernible through linguistic differentiation rather than through divisions of space. In 'The Reve's Tale', the
beloved figure, so significant in the two previous tales, has no meaning apart from that of a counter: value here is accorded to activity,
to circulation, not to the object. Despite the seeming lightness of its
comedy, the values of this tale lead to that of the Cook, a narrative
in which money determines value, and where the individual speaker
and the physical world lose significance, both swallowed up in a
system of ceaseless exchange. In 'The Cook's Tale', the desired figure
is debased and becomes a prostitute, and the pleasurable voice of the
tale itself falters into oblivion.

A scholar such as Wakelin might protest that his interest lies in
language rather than *literature*, but the fact that he chooses to omit
ideological debates taking place around and through the tale indicates that he fails to distinguish the text from 'reality', and that,
in some way, he has accepted its ideological claim to centrality, its
version of the natural. It indicates that he (unwittingly) accepts
the Reeve's ideology. Wakelin is not the only one to assume that the
tale's realism is value-free, 'natural' or 'transparent'; but realism, in
this case, is a literary quality associated with the aristocratic genre of
the *fabliau*.[9] No narrative – no voice – can escape its particular
grounding, and, in the Russian-doll construction of 'The Reve's
Tale', the northern voices of the two clerks, like all the other voices
in *The Canterbury Tales*, articulate the desire for power, and a
concern with place and with displacement. In terms of the inter-
connection of the first four tales of *The Canterbury Tales*, the place
of dialect within 'The Reve's Tale' functions as part of a narrative
displacement, just as the displacement of the miller within the tale is
part of a narrative attempt to negate and displace the tale told by the
pilgrim Miller – which in turn was itself an attempt to displace his
predecessor. David Aers, treating Volosinov as a pseudonym for
Bakhtin, notes Volosinov/Bakhtin's comment that 'Each and every
word expresses the "one" in relation to the "other". I give myself
verbal shape from another's point of view, ultimately from the point
of view of the community to which I belong.' Aers adapts this to
medieval practice: 'If linguistic, social and subjective processes are
isolated at moments in the analysis of cultural practices, this model

demands that they are ultimately understood as bound together in the structures and history of particular communities' (Aers 1988, 3, including quotation from Volosinov 1986, 86).

II. *Dialect, literature and the problem of social history*

Wakelin's concern with dialect leads him to view Chaucer's use of dialect from a particular perspective: he sees it as *evidence* of the lower status of those from outside a favoured south-east. Focusing on those aspects he finds interesting, and suppressing potential contradiction, he assesses the 'imitation' of speech from this one perspective. Yet imitated speech is not limited to the representation of regional dialect but, according to H. Marshall Leicester, occurs less dramatically at every level of the complex interplay of voices that makes up *The Canterbury Tales*: '[T]he *Canterbury Tales* is not written to be spoken as if it were a play. It is written to be read, but reads as *if* it were to be spoken. The poem is a literary imitation of oral performance' (Leicester 1980, 221). Where Wakelin considers that the students' linguistic difference marks them out as butts of social ridicule, Leicester focuses on language as a *self*-defining act, a marker of identity. From Leicester's perspective, the depiction of language within 'The Reve's Tale' locks the text into an ongoing literary debate about language and identity. Certainly readings which see John and Aleyn as foolish provincial students become difficult to sustain when faced by what they exclude. Uneasy with the conventional reading, N. F. Blake (1981) questions whether it is possible to see the use of dialect as part of a satire on the provinces. He considers this to be an anachronistic move, a case of reading modern attitudes into literature of the past. Yet he makes a similar mistake. Assuming the transhistorical relevance of current social norms, he sees the students as 'higher up the social and educational ladder' and thus assesses 'the miller [as] perhaps more provincial and certainly more boorish than the undergraduates' (1981, 29). This approach throws up as many problems as it appears to solve.

The implication of Wakelin's reading of the relation of the clerks to the miller is that the tale exemplifies the emergence of modern attitudes and class differences. In rejecting this view, Blake seems to imply a stable social hierarchy. His response is not to question class but to seek an ideologically free arena: that of 'literature'. Wakelin divorces the use of dialect from its literary context within the tale in order to transform it into historical, dialectological evidence; Blake, wishing to avoid the grand narrative of dialectology, focuses instead on the literary aspects of the tale, and similarly removes it from the social instability of its immediate historical context.[10] He suggests that the depiction of dialect within the tale is only significant as a *literary* device adopted from the French *fabliau*: 'it is customary to use dialect or linguistic quirks as a source of humour and Chaucer may have imitated this French tradition in his use of the northern dialect' (1981, 29). To Blake, the *fabliau* is a 'short, humorous and frequently bawdy story' (1981, 29), one that appears value-free, operating in a realm outside society and social change. Yet this is far from the case, most particularly among the symbolic characters to whom Chaucer gives three interconnected *fabliaux*: the Miller, the Reeve and the Cook.[11]

To expand: the thirteenth-century *fabliau* which provided the basis for these tales is widely recognized as an aristocratic medium, one which depends very much on the satirization of groups perceived as inferior. The stark realism which is employed within the tales is equally ideological, for it magnifies the gross physicality by which the lower orders are stigmatized. By constructing an unrefined world inhabited by figures dominated by various – though primarily sexual – lusts and wholly lacking in the 'spiritual' qualities through which the aristocracy idealized and justified their status, the *fabliau* degrades its characters, who are the butts of a bawdy and usually scatological humour. In the *fabliau*, frequent adulterous adventures demonstrate the inability of the lower-class figures to restrain their desire and therefore also their inability to adhere to a 'civilized' order and law.[12] Thus the comedy of the *fabliau* is aware of class division and actively promotes it. A glance at the romance, the arena in which the aristocracy presented idealized images of themselves as noble, ethical beings, indicates the extent to which the *fabliau* is rooted in the cultural politics of class. J. T. Jackson Lears's deliberation (1985) on Gramsci is particularly relevant to what I mean by the 'cultural politics of class':

Gramsci realised that a class interpretation of history does not entail a fixation on the struggle between oppressors and oppressed; rather, as Eugene Genovese has observed, 'it may reveal a process by which a ruling class successfully avoided such confrontation', and the source of that success may well be in the realm of culture. (Lears 1985, 572)

Not only as a genre, but also as a representative style (realism), the thirteenth-century French *fabliaux* serve the interests of the aristocratic class. Yet that need not mean that *Chaucer*'s use of the same genre does likewise. The place from which the *fabliaux* in *The Canterbury Tales* are spoken is clearly demonstrated within the wider frame of that text; and changing the domain in this way effects changes within the genre. Robert Hodge's fascinating discussion of the interaction of 'genre and domain' points out that 'crossing genres or domains is always an intervention at a certain point in the system, which reveals something of the system itself . . . Genres are fluid, untidy products of negotiation and struggle whose outcome is not always certain or predictable' (Hodge 1990, 35–6). And one striking characteristic of Chaucer's use of the *fabliau* is that he places it in the mouths of the very figures whom the aristocratic form was designed to humiliate and ridicule. As Derek Pearsall (1987, 42) points out, this change has 'wonderfully complicated our response' to the *fabliau*. At a stroke, aristocratic patronization is transformed into a self-reflection: a strategy perfectly in keeping with the sophisticated exploration of the relation of language to identity that Leicester sees as the preoccupation of the *Tales* as a whole.

By assessing the *fabliau* as merely a short humorous story, Blake appears to echo Wakelin's view that the literary text is both value-free and essentially unproblematic, and similarly he makes no distinction between the use of language within the text and that of everyday life. Though disagreeing with the traditional assessment of the use of dialect in 'The Reve's Tale' as a fourteenth-century attempt to mock the 'inferior' dialect of the north, Blake seems less aware of history as a determining factor in literature than is Wakelin: he accepts that dialect is comic but is unsure whether it is satiric. He turns to 'literary' questions as a way of avoiding the political, a move that denies the space of the literary as what Patterson calls 'a space of ideological opposition' (1987, 74). For Blake, literature is certainly not to be interrogated for elements that might modify predetermined assumptions about the relation of language and identity.

III. Place and displacement

'The Miller's Tale' constructs 'a space of ideological opposition' to the dominant order through its central concern with place and displacement. (This is why the Reeve is so concerned to negate its values in his tale, to emasculate its vitality through the agency of his northern students.) The Miller seeks to displace the fear and anxiety that the Knight associates with the physical and sensuous world and to replace it with celebration. One of the ways in which this is effected is through the loving detail accorded to the physical world, to the physical being of the central protagonists, and to the recurrent desire to enter (simultaneously) the inner spaces of both Alison and the house; a desire shared by the narrative and the clerks, Nicholas and Absolon. The central metaphor of 'The Miller's Tale' is that of *space*. As a carpenter, Alison's husband is a creator of spaces, who is *re*placed by Nicholas and *dis*placed into the eaves of the house; Absolon wishes to enter Alison's interior space from the exterior space of the street. In this tale, inner spaces are sweet (Nicholas's chamber; Alison's mouth), bad things are pushed outside (Alison threatening to throw stones from inside the house at Absolon on the street; Nicholas farting out of the window).

Patterson insists that the celebration of a rich physical world in 'The Miller's Tale' has a deliberate political end, that of 'subverting and mocking the very terms with which the reigning ideology sought to stigmatize and oppress peasants . . . Far from being fallen and degraded, nature here serves as a beneficent and supportive principle' (1991, 264–5). If the Miller's attempt to reclaim the value of the physical world is part of a political agenda, then the Reeve's rewriting is equally political. 'The Reve's Tale' rewrites not only its paradigm's celebration of sensuality but also its dominant metaphor. Whereas 'The Miller's Tale' sketched a varied and complex urban world (Oxford), with a focus on the physical spaces of the carpenter's house, the world of 'The Reve's Tale' is denuded of such complexity. It consists of one building (both work and living space) isolated from the town (Cambridge), and surrounded by fields and wild mares which run off, distracting the clerks' (male) workhorse.

The Reeve's rewriting is particularly evident in the new – and heightened – role accorded to *language*. Within the Miller's narrative, communication can take place without words: Alison's shuddering response when Nicholas touches her makes her verbal rejection redundant; the non-verbal 'Tehee' as she shuts the window on the shocked Absolon wonderfully conveys mischievous delight; the fart that eloquently echoes out over Absolon's face is as expressive as any words. In 'The Miller's Tale', the two clerks are divided through their relation to physicality and language: Absolon is 'somdel squaymous / Of farting' (lines 151–2) and sings in an affected manner to improve his own appearance; Nicholas is the one who farts on Absolon, and who works with Alison, exploiting biblical texts for their mutual advantage. The extended physical description of Nicholas (and the lack of such description of the carpenter) demonstrates his alliance with the equally physical Alison. The contrast with Absolon emphasizes further this alliance with the physical world. As a lodger, Nicholas's home already lies within the house, while the wandering Absolon is an outsider whose *words* may enter the house but who has no physical presence there.

'The Miller's Tale' not only reclaims nature, it reclaims the spaces of the physical world: not just the vernal imagery that associates Alison with the countryside, but the physical structure of the town itself, with its streets and its miracle plays and churchgoing; not just the town either, but the house itself, with its individual rooms, the scented musical interior associated with Nicholas, and the transformation of Alison's bedroom into a place of melody and laughter through sexual play.

In 'The Miller's Tale', the human world encompasses *unlicensed* sexual desire; its significant boundary lies within the town – specifically at Alison's shot-window – indicating the physical division of the private/erotic space of the bedchamber from the public space of the street. When Absolon sings – attempting to penetrate this boundary with his 'unnatural' voice – Alison states her own (ambiguous) desire and threatens him with a physical object – the stone:

> I love another, and elles I were to blame,
> Wel bet than thee, by Jesu, Absolon!
> Go forth thy wey, or I wol caste a ston.
>
> (lines 524–6)

Alison's colloquial speech seems at some distance from a study of dialect in 'The Reve's Tale', but it indicates the grounds on which she is characterized, grounds which 'The Reve's Tale' deliberately rewrites. The most important of these is the rewriting – and degrading – not only of nature and the pleasure of sex, but also of the human division of physical space: that which provides the ordering principle within 'The Miller's Tale'. This context clarifies why the divisions within 'The Reve's Tale' are defined through language and the opposition of movement and stasis; why the students are outsiders, uttering an alien *speech*, a dialect that reveals that they are not inhabitants of the miller's world. In the former tale, Alison has her own space and the tale circulates around that space. Nicholas manipulates biblical texts in order to achieve union with Alison in her bedroom; the clerks in the Reeve's narrative grab what they can get, manipulating the *space* of the bedroom itself.

Far from indicating the inferiority of the 'provincial' students, John and Aleyn's dialect is part of an ideological attack on those elements given value and respect within the earlier tale (which itself expresses the values of a restive peasant class). It is an attack which Blake inadvertently supports in his description of the miller as 'grasping' (1981, 29). Blake himself draws attention to the association of the clerks with the manipulation of space, though he does not think it is important. He notes that the miller seems uninterested in and unaffected by the students' dialect: '[W]e are not led to believe that because of their speech he treated them differently from the way that he would have treated other undergraduates who spoke London English' (Blake 1981, 29). He cites the miller's jibe at the students:

> ye that han lerned art;
> Ye conne by argumentes make a place
> A myle brood of twenty foot of space.
>
> (lines 202–4)

Blake considers this only as a form of excuse, an apology for the lack of room. Because he assumes that 'such comments serve only to emphasize the undergraduates' learning and to play down any northern unsophisticated ways they may have' (1981, 29), he finds this issue puzzling. Yet the passage to which he refers does not denote shame on the miller's part but rather a sense of having beaten the students, brought them down to his level: to the level of the physical world, a world which cannot be altered. But, of course, as the tale demonstrates, this is not the case: where the miller exploits existing space, the two students transform it.

It is a space ordered very crudely around the placing of sleeping areas, and therefore of erotic potential. The crucial distinction between public and private drawn in the previous tale is missing: the mill is both workplace and home, and there is no street to accommodate the boundary between two kinds of human activity. The only space outside the mill is the fen where wild horses rampage with inarticulate cries of sexual pleasure: 'wehee', as Patterson points out (1991, 275), rewrites the 'Tehee' of the coltish Alison, her exclamation now shorn of its human, humorous aspect. Where 'The Miller's Tale' celebrated the physical world through a depiction of rich and varied spaces and non-verbal communication, in 'The Reve's Tale' everything is subordinated to the language of trickery. The tale presents us with a degraded, oppressive sense of space in the cramped, smelly, noisy room (the miller's fart remains within the room; the only harmony is that of the three family members snoring in unison). The physical world of 'The Reve's Tale' is constricted and degraded, and language offers an escape from such entrapment: a perfect analogy for the students from the north, to whom the drunken family's inarticulate snoring acts as a trigger for revenge:

> Aleyn the clerk, that herd this melodye,
> He poked John, and seyde, 'slepestow?
> Herdestow ever slyk a sang er now?
>
> (lines 249–51)

Significantly, the physical delight of sex, by being rewritten in terms of an economic exchange, is brought within the remit of human law and justice. The clerks' revenge is both verbalized and understood in terms of written law: 'Som esement has lawe y-shapen us' (line 259).

Wakelin's and Blake's interpretations of the use of dialect in 'The Reve's Tale' bear out Patterson's contention that the absence of an explicit ideology leads to an 'unintended conservatism' (1987, 70). On the one hand, Wakelin's failure to recognize the literary dimension of the text reveals his blindness to the narrative construction of his own discipline; on the other hand, Blake's avoidance of the 'political' masks the hidden politics of his own approach. My own agenda is clear: to focus on the entwined relation of class and cultural meaning and, as part of that, to demonstrate the different reading that emerges when an element taken to be neutral by other approaches is recognized as a class signifier.

The ground upon which the tales are constructed is that of the physical world, the birthplace of all speaking subjects, the context within which they move, the very material of their bodies. The physical world is thus intimately caught up in the production of meaning, for no language/dialect is disembodied and universal – though the ruling class might assert that this is possible, and that it is their own speech that is universal. Patterson's claim that 'each *Tale* is . . . grounded in a speaking subject' (1991, 26) looks forward to the construction of subjectivity, but, equally, the grounding itself is important, being the particular place or class position which governs both speech and the significance of that speech. Judged in this way, the students' alien dialect not only displays their difference from the miller and his family, but also their negative relation to the place depicted in the text. Even before they speak they are characterized as having left their 'ground' behind: 'Strother / Fer in the north, I can nat telle where'. When they do speak, this forgotten space echoes through their language, defining them as mobile figures – a factor of far greater importance than either physical description or a habitation at Cambridge.

The omission of physical description or natural home is not recognized in Patterson's assessment of the narrative strategies of the *Tales*. He comments that 'Chaucer persistently filters into the narratorial description of each pilgrim an individualizing voice' (1991, 27). But there are figures who lack 'an individualizing voice'. The most individualizing element in the description of the Cook is a reference to his ulcerated shin amongst the list of his professional abilities. As he is the merchants' servant, catering to their appetites, this reference implies not only physical decay but a restricted personal mobility. The merchants are on the move; the Cook merely accompanies them, for money. The description of the Cook makes no mention of speech, his 'tale' never gets any-where. The example of the Reeve's clerks provides the other extremity, that of speech without physical description. Speech thus does not merely individuate the speaking subject, it signifies status and power.

In the case of the Reeve's miller and his family, speech functions more elaborately, for their speech mimics that of the Knight: simultaneously expressing a desire for increased status and under-cutting it through parody. This is true for both the miller (with his pride in his 'estaat of yomanrye', line 29) and his daughter (whose words parody those of a courtly lady). Within the context of *The Canterbury Tales*, there is an implicit contrast with the pilgrim Yeoman, who is given neither voice nor tale, and whose description reinforces his class position: 'Wel coude he dresse his takel yemanly' ('General Prologue', line 106).

The description of the Reeve's miller carries two entwined messages: social aspiration and unpredictable violence. His pre-occupations echo those of the warrior Knight: a concern for respect and honour, a willingness to fight, a desire to protect his women. But these symbolic values are rendered ridiculous in the physical realm of the miller. The phallic symbolism of the lordly sword is fractured into the three knives that hang suggestively around his groin (one is secreted in his hose). The description both invokes the abstract knightly ideal and explodes it through the miller's (physical) particu-larity, 'proving' through excess that the miller cannot be the 'real' thing and that he is unfit for the knightly power he desires.

In terms of the wider patterns of *The Canterbury Tales*, the Knight is the figure whose courtly romance the *pilgrim* Miller had aggres-sively attempted to 'quite' with the physicality of his *fabliau*: an attempt that implies a challenge to the Knight's authority (Patterson 1991, 244). In his reconfigurations of 'The Miller's Tale', the Reeve translates sensuous vitality into blustering overcompensation. Having an interest in keeping the system as it is, he turns signs of class defiance into marks of petty aggression, and signs of social power into marks of personal impotence.[13] Both narratives ('The Miller's Tale' and 'The Reve's Tale') register the role of millers in contemporary peasant risings; the first giving the miller a voice, the second denying the individuality of that voice by presenting it as hollow mimicry.

Demanding the term of address accorded to the dominant class, the Reeve's miller's language is perfectly in line with his portrayal as 'theef' (line 19). He desires a wife 'To saven his estaat of yomanrye' (line 29), and requires that she be addressed as 'dame' (line 36). Yet the miller cannot be dismissed out of hand as a posturing idiot (cf. Absolon in 'The Miller's Tale'). His pride in his 'estaat of yomanrye' points towards a *class* demand for increased social status, rather than an individual bid to gain admittance into the more prestigious levels of a fixed and accepted hierarchy. His horrified response to Aleyn's having sex with his daughter is rooted in an inflated awareness of position, a parody of aristocratic privilege: 'Who dorste be so bold to disparage / My doghter, that is come of swich linage?' (lines 351–2). In order to ensure the status quo it is essential that the threat posed by the miller be neutralized. For all his fabled violence, Simpkin is thoroughly beaten by both students (line 388), while his phallic paraphernalia fails to protect him from sexual humiliation: not only does John have sex with his wife, he is more virile than her husband – 'So mery a fit ne hadde she nat ful yore' (line 310).

Social aspiration and physicality find a representation also in the miller's two women: the wife's social aspiration is expressed through the red clothes that defy the sumptuary laws, the daughter is defined by a physical description that, like that of her father, both invokes and parodies the aristocratic ideal:

> This wenche thikke and wel y-growen was,
> With camuse nose and yën greye as glas;
> With buttokes brode and brestes rounde and hye,
> But right fair was hir heer, I wol nat lye.
>
> (lines 53–6)

As the next, and fertile, generation, the (apparently naked) daughter serves to focus the transgressive desires of both Church and peasantry. If her peasant-father looks to her for the future fulfilment of his dreams of increased social status, and the establishment of new lines of inheritance, so too does her priest-grandfather:

> His purpose was for to bistowe hir hye
> In-to som worthy blood of auncetrye;
> For holy chirches good moot been despended
> For holy chirches blood, that is descended.
>
> (lines 61–4)

If the priest and the miller of 'The Reve's Tale' aspire to greater status, the coming of the clerks and Aleyn's penetration of Malin ensures that this cannot happen. Aleyn's jumping into bed with Malin puts her and her family back in their subordinate places, quashing the possibility that a peasant girl might marry above her station and ally herself with a noble house. The clerks' mobility and activity expresses their masculine potency: John 'priketh harde and depe as he were mad' (line 311), while Aleyn claims to have 'thryes, in this short night, / Swyved the milleres doghter bolt-upright' (lines 345–6). And, in so doing, they crush their class rival.

The clerks' mobility is crucial to 'The Reve's Tale' on every interwoven level: their movements define the narrative structure of the tale – they move from Strother to Cambridge, from Cambridge to the mill, from the mill to the fens and back, eventually returning to Cambridge (and beyond); in terms of the social patterning of the tale, they are adept at taking others' places – the college manciple, the hoped-for aristocrat in Malin's bed, and Simpkin in bed with his (unnamed) wife;[14] finally, throughout the story itself they are continuously active – even when cursing and running after their stallion. No assessment of the students' dialect is viable without taking this vicious class comedy into account. The clerks' identity is as rooted in this mobility, this movement through and mastery over space, as it is created through their language. As Blake points out, it is the clerks' argumentational prowess, their verbal dexterity, that attracts the miller's comment, not their alien speech. Dialect thus appears to be a structural marker for the reader, a means of separating out the different selves of the two groups.

Dialect in 'The Reve's Tale' is significant because of its relation to the physical element of space: it both gestures towards and denies space. It is not a humorous incident occurring between equal individuals, who are consequently qualified by variations in speech. The degradation of the value attached to the physical world is intimately entwined with the verbal dexterity of a group out to pursue their own interests in a mobile and back-stabbing society. From a modern perspective, this devaluation of space marks the reductive fixing of the peasant class into a backwater: the provincial arena where nothing can happen.

IV. Final notes

If the traditional 'comic' reading can be used to support the notion of a medieval recognition of 'Standard English', deviations from which are to be sneered at as amusing provincialism, then the alternative reading that I propose cannot help but undermine that argument and, along with it, the practice of studying language as 'dialect'. The routine accumulation of 'information' about dialect implies the acceptance of a fixed ground from which this 'value-free' activity can take place – and that ground, this reading of 'The Reve's Tale' suggests, is the ground of class subjection, an unstable ground caught up with silences and with the silencing of alternatives.

'The Reve's Tale' articulates the subjectivity of a figure defined through his economic activity, a Reeve,[15] and, in the process, expresses the ideology of a group that seeks to keep the peasants in their place, retaining the established order as long as it is able to move upwards within it. Murray (1978, 237) points out that the intellectual élite characterized by argument and rationality 'fought for itself . . . [It] fought persons below it in the social hierarchy, to rise above them. And it fought those above, to replace them.' Picking up on Murray's discussion of the *literati*, Moore (1990, 139) writes of the 'hostility of the *clericus* to the *illiteratus, idiota, rusticus*'. Though his subject is heresy it is significant that the terms of abuse were adapted from those referring to class. One of the measures of this ideology's long-term success must be the way its particular perspective is confused with 'reality', both by traditional literary critics who seek to divorce text from context, to look only at 'the words on the page', and by dialectologists who divorce the issue of language from that of literature, thus denying literature the ambiguity which enables it to become a 'space of ideological opposition' (Patterson 1987, 74): an opposition which this discussion on the politics of space has attempted to open out.[16]

Notes

1 Text from *The Complete Works of Geoffrey Chaucer*, edited by W. W. Skeat (1912).

2 The interrelated structure of *The Canterbury Tales* is generally accepted: Donald R. Howard (1976) and Helen Cooper (1983) provide pertinent examples. H. Marshall Leicester (1990) and Lee Patterson (1991) in particular emphasize the spoken quality of the tales and the role of that speech in constructing identity.

3 'History impelled Chaucer towards the modern and he accepted the challenge by investigating not just the idea of history, as in *Anelida and Arcite* and the *Troilus*, but, in *The Canterbury Tales*, the historical world itself' (Patterson 1991, 26).

4 The clerks inhabit a world of backbiting: 'men wil us foles calle, / Bathe the wardeyn and our felawes alle, / And namely the miller' (lines 191–3); in this world the individual must take risks or fail: 'Yet has my felawe som-what for his harm; / . . . He auntred him . . . when this jape is tald another day, / I sal be halde a daf, a cokenay! / I wil aryse, and auntre it' (lines 283–9).

5 The Reeve manipulates the system to his own advantage: 'Ther was noon auditor coude on him winne' (line 594 of 'General Prologue'); 'Ther coude no man bringe him in arrerage' (line 602); 'He coude bettre than his lord purchace' (line 610).

6 Patterson (1991, 248), discussing Robert Brenner, 'The origins of capitalist development: a critique of neo-Smithian Marxism' (1977). See also S. H. Rigby (1995, 61–6), who addresses the relation of Marx to Adam Smith in his examination of various interpretations of a changing medieval economy.

7 Patterson's comment that 'every courtly poem is in effect a debate' (1992, 28) represents an approach which can be applied to Chaucer's text, which was produced in the shadow of the court, as well as to that of his friend, the Lollard knight, Sir John Clanvowe.

8 'Some texts actively engage the phenomenon of voice, exploit it, make it the centre of their discourse . . . A text of this sort can be said to be *about* its speaker' (Leicester 1980, 217).

9 'The *fabliau* is as courtly a genre as the romance – is indeed the comic and realistic side of the coin of serious and idealising romance . . . [*Fabliaux*] are aristocratic burlesques, contemptuously holding up to amusement the coarse buffooneries of lower classes and some clergy' (Brewer 1979, 298–9). (Brewer notes a history of critical discussion about the class origin of the *fabliaux* – see also note 15 below.)

10 Alexander Murray's brilliant study of social change in the Middle Ages links the bitter resentment that clerical mobility created, especially among the peasantry, to a greater social instability. He devotes a whole chapter, 'The university ladder', specifically to clerkly careerism, and two others to the relation of this emergent intellectual élite to peasants and aristocrats respectively (see Murray 1978).

11 Though I do not agree wholly with his reading of the Reeve's and the Cook's tales, Patterson's discussion ('"The Miller's Tale" and the politics of laughter', chapter 5 of 1991) of the significance of these three figures is extremely pertinent: millers were often associated with the peasants' revolts (pp.254–8); the Reeve's work gives him the status of 'an agent of seigneurial control [with] social ambitions' (p.274); as one of the 'journeymen wage labourers', the Cook is associated with 'lower-class criminality' (p.278).

12 I do not quarrel with Peter Dronke's scholarly investigation of 'The rise of the medieval *fabliau*' (in *The Medieval Poet and his World*, 1984; see especially pp.145–7), which claims that Latin evidence challenges the assumption that the aristocracy were instrumental in creating the genre. What can be seen – and this is in line with Robert Moore's analysis

(1990) of the growth of persecution during the early twelfth century – is an appropriation of that form for class purposes, purposes that come to dominate its reception and comprehension.

13 Mary Douglas's investigation of the relation between ritual pollution, taboo and the notion of sexual purity, in her *Purity and Danger: An Analysis of the Concepts of Pollution and Taboo* (1966), has been widely adapted to other circumstances. Robert Moore (1990, 100) focuses on her revelation of the way in which groups essential to the workings of society, but accorded little status, are sexualized so that the need for *social* containment can be justified as a policy of *sexual* containment. Though Douglas discusses tribal women in the Congo, Moore applies her principle to race and class. Seen from this perspective the Reeve's ridiculing of his miller's sexual prowess is a part of a class-based put-down.

14 The students appropriate the seigneurial privilege of sleeping with peasant women.

15 Rigby (1995, 74) points out that the fourteenth-century practice of replacing farmers with reeves or bailiffs 'to organise production' demonstrates the landlords' increasing interest in managing their estates for the market.

16 The work of social theorists like Edward Soja and Henri Lefebvre productively investigates the sociology of space. The analysis of another social theorist, Kevin Hetherington (1997), complements my reading of the interplay of voice and space in 'The Reve's Tale'. Where I argue that the clerks' manipulation of space through language introduces an instability to the meanings attached to the space of a restive peasantry, Hetherington notes that such ambiguity reflects the unstable conditions of modernity. Both analyses thus suggest that the clerks' introduction of alien voices can be linked to the modern dominance of the bourgeoisie.

Works cited

Aers, David. 1988. *Community, Gender, and Individual Identity: English Writing 1360-1430*. London: Routledge.

Blake, N. F. 1981. *Non-Standard Language in English Literature*. London: André Deutsch.

Brenner, Robert. 1977. The origins of capitalist development: a critique of neo-Smithian Marxism. *New Left Review*, 104 (1977), 25–82.

Brewer, D. S. 1979. The fabliaux. In Beryl Rowlands (ed.), *A Companion to Chaucer Studies*, pp.247–67. Oxford and New York City: Oxford University Press, 1979.

Chaucer, Geoffrey. [1912]. *The Complete Works of Geoffrey Chaucer*. Edited by W. W. Skeat, Oxford: Oxford University Press.

Cooper, Helen. 1983. *The Structure of 'The Canterbury Tales'*. Athens: University of Georgia Press.

Douglas, Mary. 1966. *Purity and Danger: An Analysis of the Concepts of Pollution and Taboo*. London: Routledge and Kegan Paul.

Dronke, Peter. 1984. *The Medieval Poet and his World*. Rome: Edizioni di Storia e Letteratura.

Hetherington, Kevin. 1997. *The Badlands of Modernity: Heterotopia and Social Ordering*. London: Routledge.

Hodge, Robert. 1990. *Literature as Discourse*. Cambridge: Polity Press.

Howard, Donald R. 1976. *The Idea of 'The Canterbury Tales'*. Berkeley: University of California Press.

Lears, J. T. Jackson. 1985. The concept of cultural hegemony. *American Historical Review*, 90 (1985), 567–93.

Leicester, H. Marshall. 1980. The art of impersonisation: a general prologue to *The Canterbury Tales. PMLA*, 95 (1980), 213–24.

——. 1990. *The Disenchanted Self: Representing the Subject in 'The Canterbury Tales'*. Berkeley: University of California Press.

Moore, Robert. 1990. *The Formation of a Persecuting Society*. Oxford: Basil Blackwell.

Murray, Alexander. 1978. *Reason and Society in the Middle Ages*. Oxford: Clarendon Press.

Patterson, Lee. 1987. *Negotiating the Past: The Historical Understanding of Medieval Literature*. Madison: University of Wisconsin Press.

——. 1991. *Chaucer and the Subject of History*. London: Routledge.

——. 1992. Court politics and the invention of literature: the case of Sir John Clanvowe. In David Aers (ed.), *Culture and History 1350–1600: Essays on English Communities, Identities and Writing*, pp.7–41. Hemel Hempstead: Harvester Wheatsheaf, 1992.

Pearsall, Derek. 1987. Versions of comedy in *The Canterbury Tales*. In Joerg O. Fichte (ed.), *Chaucer's Frame Tales: The Physical and the Metaphysical*, pp.35–49. Tübingen: Narr, and Cambridge: Brewer, 1987.

Rigby, S. H. 1995. *English Society in the Later Middle Ages: Class, Status and Gender*. London: Macmillan.

Volosinov, V. N. 1986. *Marxism and the Philosophy of Language*. Cambridge, Mass.: Harvard University Press.

Wakelin, Martyn F. 1977. *English Dialects: An Introduction*. Revised edition. London: Athlone Press.

3

Maintaining the Standard

CLIVE UPTON

Once I was asked to take over from another teacher, at short notice and in mid-session, two parallel teaching courses. One was entitled 'Dialectology', the other 'Sociolinguistics'. Some of my students were enrolled on both. Although the courses were half completed their syllabuses were not fully formed, and it appeared likely that, unless action was taken to clarify their contents, those students who were involved in both subjects were destined to receive a good deal of repetition. Alan Thomas, in his Preface to *Methods in Dialectology* (1988, v), reasonably refers to the 'pedant who seeks an inviolate line of demarcation' between dialectology and sociolinguistics. But I had a strong incentive to run the risk of being thought pedantic by discovering a workable separation of the two.

There are, of course, various possible definitions for both labels. One plausible split is 'separation by dimension', whereby dialectology is seen as essentially concerned with the spatial and temporal dimensions, and sociolinguistics is regarded as addressing primarily the social or speaker variables. This seems to be at the heart of Thomas's stance, since he continues:

> The defining criterion for dialectology, perhaps, is its central concern with variation in the spatial parameter and with diffusion through space and time, in addition to refinement of data by an enhanced awareness of the significance of factors of communal social structure. (Thomas 1988, v)

There is much to recommend this definition, especially if, as Robert Penhallurick suggests in 'The politics of dialectology' (1992), the social dimension is not restricted to a mere 'refining role'. It was not Thomas's task, however, to disambiguate dialectology and sociolinguistics as I necessarily had to do. And indeed it is possible to do so without declining into pedantry, locating definitions which will permit both dialectology and sociolinguistics sufficient room to embrace all their many concerns, which in the case of sociolinguistics can reasonably be taken to range widely, from the microlinguistic patterning of interpersonal communication to such macrolinguistic issues as multilingualism and language planning.

It should be acknowledged at once that, special circumstances aside, rigid disambiguation of terms is not necessary or even especially helpful to the progress of linguistics. Arguing for his own separation of terms, Trudgill (1999, 3) cites as the ultimate stance Hymes's opposition to 'the parcelling up of the human sciences into separate, labelled and competing disciplines'. Nevertheless, I had determinedly to separate dialectology and sociolinguistics if chaos was not to ensue, and order was at hand in the shape of Francis's *Dialectology: An Introduction* (1983). Here we read the following:

> It is not always easy to distinguish between the sociolinguist and the dialectologist. A rough distinction, which not all of either group would accept, is that the sociolinguist is primarily interested in the people themselves, and hence in the language for what it can reveal about them, while the dialectologist is interested in the language itself and studies the social aspects for what they can reveal about it. (p. 8)

This provides a comprehensive and comprehensible separation. Whilst the separation of the disciplines is, one would hope, never complete for the student of language variation, the *focus* of concern is most definitely different.

Interestingly, and I feel unfortunately, an arguable difference between the two disciplines pointed up by Francis is promptly blurred by his adopting 'sociolinguistic' as a modifier for 'dialectology' when needing a term for Labovian language-variation enquiries. He does this in spite of the fact that the essential focus of such studies is linguistic rather than social. More helpful for such an enquiry when the focus is linguistic is, I would maintain, 'social dialectology', that is, variation studies in which language concerns are paramount ('dialectology') but in which the language is seen in its social dimension, quantified according to various social variables and so on. If this is accepted, the label 'sociolinguistic dialectology' is left free for use at the interface of the two disciplines, where dialectology is practised with a definite view to advancing understanding of people, their relationships and interactions, that is, where the focus of the dialectologist is towards the dialect *speaker* rather than the dialect *form*.

The distinction is, I grant, a nice one. The social dialectology of Labov, Trudgill and others does provide us with insights into societies, and has led to valuable commentary on truly socio-linguistic issues. To take just one example, Trudgill's *Accent, Dialect and the School* (1975) illuminates the debate concerning policies on language varieties in education in a way that can only be done by someone with first-hand knowledge of real language-variation data. In spite of the fact that exploration of language matters can often lead on to study of its societal implications, however, observation and comment remain two separate activities which do not have to be carried on by the same practitioners.

The area which concerns us here lies in that field of sociolinguistics which I would want to call 'sociolinguistic dialectology', since it concerns the implications, in the present instance the 'political' impli-cations, which linguistic variation has for language users. It should be acknowledged at once that such concerns must necessarily feed off the findings of the dialect gatherers, be they of historical, social, or any other persuasion. It is not until the material has been found that sociolinguistic concerns can be addressed to it. Once the information has been gathered by serious researchers, however, it has a great deal of importance from a social point of view. This is so whether it was gathered in a rural or urban setting, from a representative speaker sample or from speakers restricted by age, sex, education, income, race or any other speaker variable, through the application of questionnaires or in free conversation, or according to any of the other criteria beloved of the linguistic investigator.

Central to the social importance of dialectal speech is the plain fact that it is produced by *people*, and is used by *people* as their primary means of communication. It is the vehicle which carries everything from their most humdrum everyday messages to their most intimate confessions. As such, it is very important to them, so basic to their lives that they take it for granted for much of the time, but so essential also that, when others show an interest in it or threaten it, they can be roused to passion in its advocacy or its defence. What else is it, unless it is the inadequacies of their rail service, which drives more Britons to write to the newspapers or to the radio and television stations? What language researcher in possession of even a modicum of skill has for long found it difficult to locate a willing informant from whom to elicit views on accent or vocabulary? And who has not had difficulty in disengaging from a particularly enthusiastic helper?

My own early fieldwork recordings are accompanied by a set of photographs of informants. These photographs make up for me in nostalgia what they lack in artistic or technical excellence. More importantly they act as a reminder that the linguistic data which I was engaged in collecting were inextricably bound up with the speakers who gave them to me. Encouragingly, this centrality of the dialect-speaker to our subject is recognized in a most practical and productive way in one of the particularly promising developments in our field, that of perceptual dialectology.

An assertion that dialects are spoken by people may not then be the truism which it may at first seem to be. Notwithstanding this, the fact that the linguistic forms which comprise a dialect *mean* something to the user over and above the literal value of the utterances into which they are formed can, of course, be ignored quite legitimately by the historical or traditional or social dialectologist, for whom the medium is the focus of attention. But, for the dialectologist who chooses to inject a truly sociolinguistic element into her or his work, it cannot be ignored and must indeed remain central. It is this dimension, rather than any assertion of the existence of exceptions to the description, which gives the principal lie to Chambers and Trudgill's categorization of the Survey of English Dialects (SED) informants as 'non-mobile older rural males', or NORMs (1998, 29 and elsewhere). For all that such informants were not selected according to sampling techniques informed by modern social scientific criteria, but were chosen somewhat randomly as possible representatives of a specially targeted and narrow speaker-group, they were first and foremost individual speakers, whose possession of the language was as legitimate, and as precious, as that of any others.

Yet in spite of the validity of such an observation, which I think we would all affirm to some degree, we have to confront a singular fact concerning it. Notwithstanding the great importance which individual speakers attach to their own speech-forms and to the speech-forms of their community, it is our common experience that anything other than that set of sounds, lexical items and grammatical structures that are associated with a 'standard' form of the language are regarded as being less than wholly acceptable in society beyond a speaker's immediate speech-group. This is the frequently voiced intuition of the native speaker, and of course there is a rich sociolinguistic literature concerning attitudes to language which documents the issue. The intra-language diglossic situation is much more than simply an interesting linguistic phenomenon, or even a mild social irritant. The existence of a standard, and of divergence (and degrees of divergence) from it, has a bearing on the fabric of society at a very fundamental level, deeply touching many facets of our lives.

We might all agree that a dialectologist with sociolinguistic interests can legitimately lay claim to the study of non-standard varieties. But what of the standard variety itself? Are we justified in regarding the standard variety as a dialect, and thus as the stuff of dialectological scrutiny?

'Standard' is often used as a modifier for 'language', less often as a modifier for 'dialect'. It is not unusual to read an authoritative statement such as the following by Abercrombie:

I have used the word *dialect* for any form of English which differs from Standard English in grammar, syntax, vocabulary, and of course in pronunciation too, though a difference in pronunciation alone is not enough to make a difference in dialect . . . Some people speak Standard English with an accent, and some speak it without. (1951, reprinted in Petyt 1980, 17)

This notion of a standard form of language which is devoid of accent or other dialectal features is still voiced by linguists, including dialectologists. Joseph, whose *Eloquence and Power* (1987) is, I feel, essential reading on the matter of the standard, writes that a goal of his book is 'to investigate what it is that sets standard *languages* apart from non-standard *dialects*' (my emphases; 1987, 19). The Cox report into English-language teaching in British schools asserts that 'Standard English is an international *language* used throughout the world' (though it elsewhere asserts that 'Linguists generally define Standard English as a dialect') (National Curriculum English Working Group 1988, sections 4.5, 4.9). This is, of course, the popular view of the matter too.

Set against this is the view of dialect held by McDavid allowing the label to attach to *any* distinct language variety:

> a *dialect* simply defined as a variety of a language, generally mutually intelligible with other varieties of that language, but set off from them by a unique complex of features of pronunciation, grammar and vocabulary. Dialect, thus used, is not a derogatory term but a descriptive one . . . (McDavid, in Kretzschmar 1979, 159)

Here *all* varieties of a language are dialectal varieties. Differences are of form, status and function. Thus the stuff of dialectology is the study of any and all varieties, standard and non-standard, which go to make up the language.

The tendency to equate the standard with a language, of which the non-standard forms are the dialects, can be seen to stem at least in part from a simple looseness in the way such terms are applied. As evidence I offer one example, to which others can probably add more. Ronald Wardhaugh, in his *Introduction to Sociolinguistics* (1998), writes: 'Many *languages*, while not dead yet, nevertheless are palpably dying . . . For example, the French *dialects* spoken in the Channel Islands . . . are rapidly on their way to extinction' (my emphases; p.34). The apparent equating of 'standard' and 'language' in the inconsistent pseudo-linguistic Cox report can perhaps be attributed to this same tendency.

If the disagreement were only about the use of a word, 'language' or 'dialect', to denote a language-form, I would see no problem. However, the terms are so loaded that I prefer not to set 'language' against 'dialect' which, thus compared, inevitably carries the force of '*sub*-standard' as well as 'non-standard'.

But are we justified in descrying a separation of dialects or language varieties into standard and non-standard at all? I believe we are, since, as I have already said, it is our common experience that, whether we approve or not, certain forms of speech are judged to be less satisfactory than others in our (British) society. Joseph (1987, 1–2) points out that unevenness in the power wielded by communities which hold together as what he calls a 'unitary region' (paralleling Haugen's 'nation' and Fishman's 'nationality') will result in the dialect of a dominant community becoming synecdochic, elevated above the rest and subsuming other varieties as sub-varieties of itself. This process is of course observable for British

English in the historical and continuing dominance of the dialects of the extreme south-east Midlands over those of other British regions. The south-east of England is traditionally the seat of the court and government, and home of the two oldest English universities, and continuing cultural, political and economic trends seem likely to maintain its supremacy in many areas of national life.

That the process of linguistic dominance does not stop with one dialect or group of dialects acquiring more prestige than the rest is readily observable. In due course the prestige dialect can become *the* dialect, the *standard* dialect, and thus, in the view of many linguists and most lay people, the *language*, with other varieties being accorded the lesser status, that of dialects. This polarization of the varieties, inevitable though it may seem to be, leads to most unfortunate consequences, from which commentators on and describers of the language are not immune but in the face of which they should strive to raise a voice of good sense.

We might usefully study the force and consequences of the trend by looking at just two of what Joseph identifies to be the *functions*, in Kloss's terms the *Ausbau* features, of the standard variety. These are that the standard 'language' tends to be seen both as the marker or badge of the powerful and as the symbol of formality and solemnity in society.

Concerning the former, it can be readily seen that possession of the standard confers power, its acquisition bringing undoubted benefits for the acquirer. Joseph (1987, 44) quotes Otto Jespersen writing in 1925:

> [T]he parents scarcely ever succeed in talking the Standard Language quite naturally, but the children can attain to it. And this is to their advantage, not merely materially, because they can more easily obtain positions in society which now – whether one approves it or not in the abstract – are given by preference to people whose speech is free from dialect, but also because they thus escape being looked down on on account of their speech and are therefore saved from many unpleasant humiliations. Apart from all this, merely by reason of their way of speaking they have better chances of coming in contact with others and getting a fuller interchange of ideas.

I would not quarrel with this as a statement of fact. I would not challenge the inevitability of there being forms of language to which people will aspire in order to progress smoothly in society. And of course there are undoubted benefits to be had from the existence of the standard, amongst which I would cite its provision of a firm pedagogic foundation and the creative possibilities of rule-breaking which standard 'rules' allow. But we may remain uneasy on both social and linguistic grounds that the standard rides as high as it does in popular estimation, and in the estimation of many specialist commentators too.

That there is a social down-side to the fact of varietal hierarchy is apparent in its divisiveness, people being set apart from one another on the purely external and ultimately unhelpful grounds of possession of this or that dialect. More subtly, it is acknowledged by Joseph, when he quotes Brakel as pointing out,

> By sanctioning class transcendence through the insistence on rites of passage and the performance of ritual, including the learning of the standard language, the leisure class assists the power élite in skimming off the most dynamic yet docile elements of the underpriviledged [*sic*] classes for membership in the leisure class. This strengthens the élite both by adding 'new blood' and by depleting the lower classes of their most favored members. (Brakel, in Joseph 1987, 44)

This may seem to be a somewhat extreme view – Joseph calls it 'overtly abstract and idealistic' – but there is surely much truth in it. It is akin to the assertion made in a radio programme that I heard at about the time when I first read the passage, in which it was maintained that the cause of Black rights in the United States had suffered through desegregation, since many potential Black leaders had entered the middle class and had thus acquired an interest in maintaining the status quo. The divisiveness inherent in the existence of a synecdochic dialect is compounded as speakers yield to the understandable urge to possess it.

Concerning the second *Ausbau* feature frequently exhibited by the standard variety, that of its being the voice of solemnity in our culture, I might usefully quote D. J. Enright, who wrote, in support of an attack which HRH the Prince of Wales had earlier made on the use of everyday language for religious purposes: 'Churchmen ought to realise, and acknowledge, that the more "understandable" you make God, the more fatuous or foul you make him . . . Remove mystery and you are well on the way to discrediting and then demolishing religion' (Enright 1989). With the elevation of the standard in this way, and with its use as a divisive social marker, being the often jealously guarded possession of an élite, a brake is placed on the possible fertilization of the old by the new to the detriment of both the medium and the message. The élite and the conservative have a vested interest in holding to forms which are removed from the everyday experience of the majority of the population and which, being thus removed, prove elusive of emulation. We can observe the entrenchment of different speech-groups manifesting itself in a purely synchronic assessment of their speech-forms, these tending to be regarded as imbued with qualities of 'purity' or 'rightness'. Our training as linguists may tell us that such assessments are quite false, but that does not prevent many commentators and educators, swayed no doubt by the 'realities' of today rather than by linguistic truths, from adopting a similar stance.

In this matter concerning the linguistic standard and non-standard, we are clearly on contentious ground, where the socio-linguist is obliged to address issues of the deepest importance. And, of course, if the standard is regarded as a standard *dialect*, as I think it should be, the sociolinguistic dialectologist, with an overview of a range of varieties, has this issue as a fundamental concern. The opposing views with which we are concerned are neatly summarized as follows by Downes (1998, 45):

[T]he question 'What is a language?' is answerable in many ways. It depends on the context in which one approaches the question. From one set of perspectives, a language is a *dynamic process*, a changing continuum in many dimensions. From another, it is an *institutionalized entity* deeply identified with the life of a society and intricately involved in its patterns of power and its political and historical development. From this second institutional point of view, a language is a *codified set of norms* in which the heterogeneity, the dynamic ongoing processes of variability and change are repressed from consciousness. The codified set of norms is imposed on the ongoing variability and change. A language seems stable and thing-like to the imagination. From the former dynamic point of view a description of a language would include *all its variant forms and the dynamics of change*. From the institutional point of view a language would appear to consist of *unchanging, invariant structures*. These are important issues within the methodology of linguistics itself. Linguists' intuitions about the object of study cannot but be affected by standardization.

Dialectological debate is full of descriptions of the dynamic existence of apparently non-standard features of language, and of their historical existence as standard forms. The dialectologist has as a duty the injection of such insights into language description, to help to ensure that forces that would ossify the language do not succeed and that language descriptions do justice to linguistic realities rather than to linguistic reaction.

For the remainder of this essay I should like to turn to a consideration of the particular place which Received Pronunciation (RP) has in discussions about standardization. We must of course recognize at once that there is a sense in which matters of accent are peripheral to a discussion of a standard, in that, as countless commentators note, it is possible to speak a standard variety in a non-standard accent. Nevertheless, the severance of accent from other linguistic features is never complete, particularly when assessments of 'correctness' are the primary objective. RP stands in the same relationship to regional and social British accents as Standard English grammatical and lexical features do to their non-standard equivalents. And if British-English speakers are being characterized by their speech they are arguably more likely to be placed by accent than by any other feature.

When a single model is being sought for British-English pronunciation, RP is the obvious choice, being 'a standard of pronunciation which is generally considered correct and is also used as a model for the teaching of English to foreigners' (Upton et al. 1987, 4). A model labelled 'RP' has long been the norm in British-English pronouncing and general dictionaries and in language-teaching classrooms. In this regard transcribers of British-English pronunciation, with access to a generally agreed model for description, may be considered to be more fortunate than transcribers of United States American pronunciation, for which, as my American collaborator William Kretzschmar argues (in the Introduction to Upton et al. forthcoming), no nationwide model can readily be identified.

However, problems for the transcriber begin rather than end with the choice of RP as the model, since it is not possible to justify the choice of model for British-English pronunciation simply by claiming that one has chosen RP. As Daniel Jones (1969, 13(note)), like many other commentators, has made clear, RP is not and was not formerly one monolithic accent: there are variations between the pronunciations of individuals who could legitimately lay claim to an RP accent.

Within a range of accents that are RP, two essential trends, which have been termed 'U-RP' and 'mainstream RP' (by Wells 1982, 279) or 'marked' and 'unmarked' (by Honey, 1989, 38), are to be distinguished. The one variety ('U' or 'marked') is an accent which, when heard by most native speakers of British English, leads to the user being judged old-fashioned, affected or pretentious. The other ('mainstream' or 'unmarked') is an accent which, for native speakers, carries connotations of education and sophistication but no especially narrow regional overtones and certainly no serious negative judgements. With obvious idiolectal variations, it is the accent we hear used by most national radio and television newsreaders and by very many middle-aged and younger professional people. It might loosely be labelled 'broadcast RP' if yet another label were to be thought desirable: it is reasonable to maintain, however, that since it is 'mainstream' and 'unmarked' it can legitimately lay claim to the RP label without qualification. This variety of the accent contrasts strongly with the 'U' or 'marked' accent of the earlier generation of newsreaders and of conservative (often older) RP speakers generally.

In spite of the acknowledged existence of socially restricted and more broadly based RP varieties, it is the former which has tended to characterize many descriptions of RP. Rather than being regarded as referring to a universal standard to which a large number of speakers around the country can claim at least partial access, the RP label has undeniably come to be associated restrictively with older middle- and upper-class speakers in the south-east of England, with Honey estimating his unmarked RP as the possession of some 3 per cent of the population (1989, 79). That is, it is aligned exclusively with a restricted form of the synecdochic British dialect. It is interesting to speculate on why this may be so, and, although it by no means furnishes a completely satisfying answer, Joseph's assertion that 'It is in the interests of the powerful and prestigious to develop means of keeping their language difficult of attainment' appears to apply to matters of phonology as it does to the matters of grammar and graphology to which he specifically refers (1987, 43).

The insecurity which accompanies this élitism is well presented by Philip Howard (1989) in a response in *The Times* to Prince Charles's views:

It is noticeable that the grumblers about the state of the English language are all white, almost all men, almost all middle-class, and all middle-aged, temperamentally if not temporally. They find themselves surrounded by new ideas, new language, new culture, new and younger rivals, and a new world they find threatening. The only thing they feel qualified to pontificate about is the English language.

To uphold a model which is far removed from the natural speech-sounds of the majority of speakers, and which is in addition likely to be stigmatized according to the system of inverted snobbery still prevalent in Britain, is to ensure that RP will be the safe preserve of an élite and will not become the possession of even a sizeable minority of native British-English speakers.

In order to correct a situation where the British pronunciation model is the possession of a small minority restricted in terms of age, class and region, a younger, unmarked RP is that which provides the model in *The New Shorter Oxford English Dictionary* (1993), *The Concise Oxford English Dictionary* 9th and 10th editions (1995, 1999), and *The New Oxford Dictionary of English* (1998), and in the pronouncing dictionary on which I am working (*The Oxford Dictionary of Pronunciation for Current English* (*ODP*), forthcoming). My intention is to describe for the user that accent which will be most widely acceptable, as well as most intelligible, to native British-English speakers, and to which the speech of very many of them will in turn approximate. The model is an accent which is not regionally centred or redolent of class. Unlike the model more usually described, which is based on the speech of a very small group of older, privileged Britons having strong connections with, if not residence in, the south-east of England, speech conforming to this new model can be heard spoken by a wide range of natives of many parts of the country, with a wide variety of professional backgrounds (though generally with a higher than average level of education). Note that the linking of accent to the concept of social class is avoided here. 'Class', when considered from a linguistic point of view, has rightly been described by Lesley Milroy as 'a *proxy* variable covering distinctions in life-style, attitude and belief, as well as differential access to wealth, power and prestige' (1987, 101). Assigning a precise 'social class' label according to accent is an increasingly unreliable procedure in Britain.

Implicit in the espoused British-English model, then, is the view that a larger group of people can lay claim to possession of an RP accent than has often hitherto been acknowledged. Each word to be transcribed must be considered with this in mind, and each transcription must be descriptive of a pronunciation which would be judged to be unexceptionable by native speakers of British English generally. As a result of this policy, I would allow certain regularly occurring pronunciation features, which have frequently to date been ignored or marked prescriptively, to be now judged as established features of RP. Notable examples of such features are [-tʃ-] in place of [-tj-] and [-dʒ-] in place of [-dj-] in such words as *Tuesday* and *reduce*. Since it is considered that they are very frequent in RP as well as in the non-standard accents, both [tʃ] and [tj], [dʒ] and [dj] transcriptions are allowed in my descriptions.

Another very significant feature judged worthy of inclusion in the model is that of 'intrusive' *r*. Intrusive *r* is that 'linking' *r* which is unhistorical and which is therefore not supported by orthography. For example, the phrase *law and order* is in British English frequently /lɔːr ən(d) ɔːdə/. Long condemned by teachers of pronunciation, intrusive *r* is nevertheless a firmly established feature of today's mainstream RP. Wells makes the point that its avoidance is a feature of 'speech-conscious adoptive-RP', that is, the RP of those who, not being native RP speakers, self-consciously attempt the accent and in consequence produce a mannered and somewhat artificial variety (1982, 284–5).

The range of pronunciations 'allowable' in the description of RP presented in the dictionary is therefore somewhat greater than that in the transcriptions of more prescriptive pronouncing and general dictionaries, the criterion for inclusion being what is heard to be used by educated, non-regionally marked speakers rather than what is 'allowed' by a preconceived model. In addition to requiring the inclusion of some hitherto rejected variants, this policy of recording a modern model has necessitated changes being made to existing RP transcription conventions. The major changes are outlined in the following paragraphs.

The RP vowel sound in *apple* or *hand* has conventionally, though not universally, been transcribed using [æ]. However, it is noticeable that the vowel has in recent years come to be articulated in a more open position, so that [a] is now a more accurate choice of symbol.

That there is growing recognition of this change in the English-language teaching community in Britain and abroad is indicated by recent correspondence in *English Today*, on which Edmund Weiner of the *Oxford English Dictionary* and I have commented (Weiner and Upton 2000). The use of the more open vowel is an RP change which, it has been pointed out by Wells, is carrying British pronunciation further away from American, where [æ] is generally found (1982, 291–2). It is interesting to speculate that perhaps the overwhelming dominance of [a] in the non-standard British-English dialects may be one reason for its pre-eminence in today's RP (see for example Map Ph1 in Orton et al., *The Linguistic Atlas of England*, 1978).

I also believe that short [a] should be shown as a variant of long [ɑ:], representing *a* before a voiceless fricative [s], [f], and [θ] (for example in *last*, *staff*, *bath*), and before a nasal [n] and [m] + consonant (for example in *dance*, *sample*). Possession of this variant is often the only factor distinguishing a north-British RP speaker from her or his south-British counterpart, and RP is not to be considered an exclusively southern-British phenomenon.

[ʌɪ], with a start-point at centralized Secondary Cardinal Vowel (SCV) 6, is the transcription which I regularly prefer for the diphthong of *nice*, *try*, *horizon*. The start-point for the unmarked British diphthong is judged to be now characteristically in the area of the vowel of *but* (half-open, back centralized), rather than the low front-ish position [a], Primary Cardinal Vowel (PCV) 4, which is the start-point characteristically adopted by more traditional transcribers. My notation was, I believe, first used by MacCarthy in *The Teaching of Pronunciation* (1978, 92).

The mainstream vowel sound of *square*, *hair* is today normally a long monophthongal [ɛ:], although it is sometimes attended by an off-glide, particularly in a stressed final syllable. A full diphthong [ɛə] in this position should now be taken to be especially a feature of a marked variety of RP. The diphthong is even more rarely heard in a compound such as *hairpiece* than it is in the simplex *hair*.

In addition to these transcriptions of recent developments in RP, I also use two composite symbols, [ɨ] and [ʉ], to represent [ɪ] or [ə] and [ʊ] or [ə] respectively. It is often recognized that [ɪ] and [ʊ], when they occur in unstressed or weakly stressed syllables, are regularly 'reduced' to [ə], schwa, by many RP speakers. The reduced vowel [ə] is even more a feature of American English in certain contexts for [ɪ], though less so for [ʊ]. The IPA (International Phonetic Alphabet) convention of 'barring' to signify centralization of high vowels and retraction of front vowels is a convenient way of showing this, and has been adopted for this feature. Whenever the barred symbols are used it is to be taken that both [ɪ] and [ə] for [ᵻ], or [ʊ] and [ə] for [ᵿ], are acceptable. This of course has some considerable similarity to the barring of PCVs 1 and 8, [i] and [u], practised particularly by phoneticians in the United States – see for example Kreidler's *The Pronunciation of English* (1989).

The table below shows some of the major situations in which the composite symbols for reduced vowels are used to show the possible RP choices.

	ODP transcription
falsITY	ᵻti
happILY	ᵻli
responsIBLE	ᵻbl
terrIBLY	ᵻbli
theatrICAL	ᵻkl
pinnACE	ᵻs
appendicitIS	ᵻs
beautiFUL	f(ᵿ)l
notED	ᵻd
risES	ᵻz

Although I have invoked the findings of the Survey of English Dialects in this brief outline of my remodelled RP, I would not wish to give the impression that the model has been constructed from some kind of synthesis of the accents of non-standard British English. Such an exercise would fly in the face of the linguistic and social realities of Britain, where RP is a decided reality of the accent model. (Kretzschmar is both able and required to create a synthe-sized model for the United States, of course, operating as he is in a quite different social, geographical and linguistic situation.) But a point that *can* be made for British English is that it is in some instances possible to descry a feature in non-standard accents which is so dominant that it can be expected to have an influence on the standard, either providing it with an acceptable variant or, as in the case of [a], with the new, younger, dominant form. Note that Survey of English Dialects fieldwork largely took place in the 1950s, when [æ] was undeniably current RP: decades of increasing mass communications and social and geographical mobility can readily account for the acceptance of a hugely dominant non-standard form into the standard accent, even into that used by younger members of the royal family.

The other point which should be made is that, accepting the premise that the standard, like the non-standard, is a dialect, this remodelling of RP is legitimate work for the dialectologist. The knowledge that accents change provides impetus for the initial enquiry and generates the misgivings concerning existing long-standing descriptions. The same observational and analytical methods are used for critical appraisal of the RP model as are used for any other accent, and the same techniques of transcription of course apply for the production of the new model. Further, if the dialectologist has a sociolinguistic direction, she or he is virtually obliged to address critically the matter of the synecdochic standard dialect in all its dimensions, since the power of the standard in societal terms is immense, and the non-standard cannot be considered sociolinguistically without being compared to and contrasted with it. Addressing RP as I have, and seeing that the acceptable unmarked accent is quite different on several counts from that presented in existing works and numerous teaching courses, I have two choices. I can accept as the standard an accent which is patently outmoded, the possession now of a speaker-group increasingly limited in terms of age and class and even, perhaps, of geographical range. Or, granting the need for an accent model such as that already in part outlined, unmarked and therefore regarded by the majority of native speakers as unexceptionable, I can redescribe, and transcribe according to the redescription. It will be apparent which option I have taken. It would of course have been pointless to transcribe according to the earlier model anyway, since that is already well represented elsewhere.

Turning at last to the title of this essay, the dual force that I give to the word 'maintaining' should be clear. A standard dialect, and the RP accent which is part of it, will inevitably remain, and one can see good reasons why that should be so. That it should be kept in good condition, serviceable for the needs of the whole community and others beyond rather than for an unrepresentative group, is, I hope, a goal for which the dialectologist can reasonably aim.

Works cited

Abercrombie, D. 1951. RP and local accent. *The Listener*, 6 September 1951, reprinted in Petyt 1980, 17.

Chambers, J. K. and Peter Trudgill. 1998. *Dialectology*. 2nd edition. Cambridge: Cambridge University Press.

Downes, William. 1998. *Language and Society*. 2nd edition. Cambridge: Cambridge University Press.

Enright, D. J. 1989. Tide of pollution that engulfs our language. *The Observer*, 24 December 1989.

Francis, W. N. 1983. *Dialectology: An Introduction*. London: Longman.

Honey, John. 1989. *Does Accent Matter? The Pygmalion Factor*. London: Faber and Faber.

Howard, Philip. 1989. Delusions of grammar. *The Times*, 21 December 1989.

Jones, Daniel. 1969. *An Outline of English Phonetics*. 9th edition. Cambridge: Heffer.

Joseph, John Earl. 1987. *Eloquence and Power: The Rise of Language Standards and Standard Languages*. London: Frances Pinter.

Kreidler, Charles W. 1989. *The Pronunciation of English*. Oxford: Basil Blackwell.

Kretzschmar, William A., Jr. (ed.). 1979. *Dialects in Culture: Essays in General Dialectology by Raven I. McDavid, Jr*. Alabama: University of Alabama Press.

MacCarthy, Peter. 1978. *The Teaching of Pronunciation*. Cambridge: Cambridge University Press.

Milroy, Lesley. 1987. *Observing and Analysing Natural Language: A Critical Account of Sociolinguistic Method*. Oxford: Basil Blackwell.

National Curriculum English Working Group [Chairman: Brian Cox]. 1988. *English for Ages Five to Eleven*. London: Department of Education and Science.

Orton, Harold, Stewart Sanderson and John Widdowson (eds.). 1978. *The Linguistic Atlas of England*. London: Croom Helm.

Penhallurick, Robert. 1992. The politics of dialectology. *Lore and Language*, 9, 2 (1990, but published 1992), 55–68.

Petyt, K. M. 1980. *The Study of Dialect: An Introduction to Dialectology*. London: André Deutsch.

Thomas, Alan R. (ed.). 1988. *Methods in Dialectology: Proceedings of the Sixth International Conference held at the University College of North Wales, 3rd-7th August 1987*. Clevedon, Avon: Multilingual Matters.

Trudgill, Peter. 1975. *Accent, Dialect and the School*. London: Edward Arnold.

——. 1999. Dialect contact, dialectology and sociolinguistics. *Cuadernos de Filóloga Inglesa*, 8, 1–8. (Reprinted from Kingsley Bolton and Hellen Kwok (eds.), *Sociolinguistics Today: International Perspectives*. London: Routledge, 1992.)

Upton, Clive, William A Kretzschmar and Rafal Konopka. Forthcoming. *The Oxford Dictionary of Pronunciation for Current English*. Oxford: Oxford University Press.

Upton, Clive, Stewart Sanderson and John Widdowson. 1987. *Word Maps: A Dialect Atlas of England*. London: Croom Helm.

Wardhaugh, Ronald. 1998. *An Introduction to Sociolinguistics*. 3rd edition. Oxford: Basil Blackwell.

Weiner, Edmund, and Clive Upton. 2000. [hat], [hæt], and all that. *English Today*, 61, volume 16, 1 (January 2000), 44–6.

Wells, J. C. 1982. *Accents of English*. Three volumes. Cambridge: Cambridge University Press.

4

Purpose, Theory and Method in English Dialectology: Towards a More Objective History of the Discipline

GRAHAM SHORROCKS

The basic epistemological assumption that underlies this chapter is that the notions *purpose* and *theory* are not altogether separable. *Theory* may be defined with Verhaar (1970, 42) as the framework within which an explanation is attempted. This framework is *systematic* and highly *explicit* in character (Verhaar 1970, 42; Chao 1970, 15), but it is also *a prioristic* because of the influence of the *frame of reference* (Verhaar 1970, 43).[1] The latter includes existing theory, which suggests new research tasks and methods by which those tasks might be accomplished. However, the frame of reference, which precedes any study, also includes the dialectologist's purpose(s). Thus, one might wish to carry out a diachronic study to examine sound changes, or a comparative study for use in education, or a detailed synchronic study for use in speech therapy, and so on (Shorrocks 1981, 32). These would be very different pieces of work, but I would consider them to be equally valid undertakings. Purpose, here, is paramount.[2] In this essay, I want to look at some of the purposes that seem to have underlain work on English dialects down through the ages; to suggest that in the 1960s, 1970s and early 1980s many lost sight of the link between purpose on the one hand and theory and method on the other; and to advocate a need to make the concept *purpose* fundamental in our historiography. *Dialectology* cannot be so narrowly defined as some writers in recent decades would have us believe.

Scientific linguistics, by common consent, did not begin until the nineteenth century, and so there was no *scholarly tradition* of work in dialectology until that same century. Our knowledge of non-standard dialects during the sixteenth, seventeenth and eighteenth centuries therefore derives from spellings in documents; from the use of non-standard dialect in literature; from early local glossaries; and from the comments of grammarians and orthoepists, whose main concern was, of course, the standard variety. However, in drawing attention to what they considered incorrect usage, they have given us a certain amount of information about other dialects.

Wakelin (1994, 34–42) included specimens of early comment on dialects, which are to be seen against the background of the rising standard variety and Renaissance nationalism, with its new-found interest in one's own language and its history. (Cf. the former importance of Latin as the language of culture and learning.) Interest in the English language seems to have been historical from the outset: it was a part of the wider interest in antiquities. Wakelin (1994, 36) noted that the Society of Antiquaries was founded in 1572; and a further boost came from the founding of the Royal Society in 1645. The early dialect glossaries were inspired by such antiquarian interests. No doubt the conservative tendencies of many of the regional dialects were felt to be interesting, and the dialectal evidence valuable for the light that it might throw on the history of standard English and on older texts, though for perhaps most antiquarians non-standard dialect was, as Levitt (1989, 9) suggested, something of a curiosity, and their collections are characterized by 'a sentimental, kindly but essentially patronising spirit'. The close link obviously felt to exist between the ancient and the dialectal is made explicit in the titles of two mid-nineteenth-century diction-aries: Halliwell's *Dictionary of Archaic and Provincial Words* and T. Wright's *Dictionary of Obsolete and Provincial English*. Halliwell (1847, vii) had no doubts about his own motivations: 'So many archaisms are undoubtedly still preserved by our rural population, that it was thought the incorporation of a glossary of provincialisms would render the work a more useful guide than one restricted to known archaisms.' He wrote that 'the only sufficient reason for preserving' provincial words was 'the important assistance they continually afford in glossing the works of our early writers'.

It is clear that a literary strand may be discerned, interwoven with the antiquarian, linguistic and nationalist threads. Thus, long before Halliwell, Nowell's *Vocabularium Saxonicum* cited non-standard words to illuminate Old English words and thereby the texts from which they were drawn.[3] More generally, many of the specimens of county dialects, which were meant to provide a sample of the local speech and were often furnished with glossaries, no doubt were intended to serve literary and linguistic ends at one and the same time. Instruction and entertainment were not felt to be mutually exclusive; indeed, humour was very much to the fore in works such as John Collier's *A View of the Lancashire Dialect*.[4]

A further motivation for dialect study in the eighteenth and nineteenth centuries was a religious one. Whitehall (1933, 261–2) drew attention to the role played by the clergy from 1700 onwards in furthering interest in dialect. In an effort to understand their parishioners better, clergymen began to learn local dialects. Such knowledge helped them perform their educational and pastoral duties better. Whitehall (1933, 262) commented:

> From this point it was an easy step to scholarly interest in dialectology and the sponsoring of dialect publications. Under clerical support dialect study and dialect literature flourished until the economic upheavals of the Industrial Revolution brought about the influx of a strong current toward secularisation.

Social motivations may also tie in with both religious and literary motivations. There is evidence of a new concern for the social, economic and moral conditions of working people in writings such as those of Elizabeth Gaskell. In *Mary Barton*, a number of the dialect words are glossed, provided with etymologies or linked through quotations to earlier literature. The Revd William Gaskell, Mrs Gaskell's husband, provided this scholarly information, and his *Two Lectures on the Lancashire Dialect* were appended to the fifth edition of *Mary Barton* (1854). In *Mary Barton* we see evidence of linguistic, literary, social and religious motivations combined. Also, the very rapid process of urbanization contingent upon industrialization produced large, working-class populations in the towns and cities of Lancashire and Yorkshire, creating a market for dialect literature and thereby providing further stimulus to dialect study. Dialect writing is still carried out today by members of such societies as the Lakeland Dialect Society (*The Journal of the Lakeland Dialect Society*, 1939–in progress), the Yorkshire Dialect Society (*Transactions of the Yorkshire Dialect Society*, 1897–in progress) and the Lancashire Authors' Association (founded 1909, and continues to this day, publishing a quarterly journal called *The Record*).

That the linguistic level of chief concern before Ellis (1889) was the lexical is understandable. Grammar was not a pre-eminent concern within language study compared with more recent times – and particularly not *de*scriptive grammar. The eighteenth-century grammatical tradition was conditioned by the Classical paradigm and was *pre*scriptive, and most people probably thought dialectal grammatical forms deviant – in the same way that dialect phonology was held to be a perversion of the standard. Thus, Edmund Coote in the late sixteenth century censured dialectal pronunciations, but was prepared to accept distinctive dialect words 'if they be peculiar termes, and not corrupting of words'.[5] Similarly, when John Collier submitted his *A View of the Lancashire Dialect* to the *Gentleman's Magazine*, they refused the work as a whole, publishing only a 'Vocabulary of the Lancashire dialect', which was introduced thus:

> We have received a DIALOGUE in the *Lancashire Dialect*, but as the peculiarity of it consists chiefly in a corrupt pronunciation of known words with few originals, and as the subject is dry and unentertaining[!], we shall only give a vocabulary of all the provincial real words, with some of the corruptions, as a specimen; and add a few lines of the performance.[6]

In refusing the dialogue because 'the peculiarity of it consists chiefly in a corrupt pronunciation of known words with few originals', the *Gentleman's Magazine* showed the then usual antiquarian interest in distinctive lexical items, and the equally usual condemnation of dialectal pronunciations of words also existing in standard English as corruptions. (Such views are, of course, still to be found in our schools and in society at large.) Phonetics was not well developed until the later part of the nineteenth century; descriptive grammar had yet to appear; and so it was lexis that held centre stage for a long period.

Comparative philology, as it developed in Germany especially, drew some of its inspiration from German Romanticism, which had not only a sense of history and nationalism, and of language as the essence of national identity,[7] but also a concept of the simplicity and purity of the *Volk*, who were felt to be closer to nature. Delbrück (1989 [1880], 33) noted that Grimm's Grammar had shown us that induction was essential to the establishment of a law, and that the latter's method had 'increased the esteem for what can be called the "natural condition" [*Naturzustand*] of language, securing to the

so-called "dialects" their proper position beside the written language
. . .' Delbrück was clearly aware of the significance of non-standard
material for linguistic theory:

> We must mention in conclusion that those scholars who advocate
> the infallibility of phonetic laws have often emphasized the fact that the
> natural constitution of language is not manifested in the cultivated
> tongues [*Kunstsprachen*], but in the dialects of the people. The guiding
> principles for linguistic research should accordingly be deduced, not
> from the obsolete written languages, but chiefly from the living popular
> dialects of the present day. (1989, 61)

The Romantics, then, were interested in both folklore and folk
speech, and nineteenth- and twentieth-century German work on the
English language has included historical works that incorporate
non-standard materials,[8] as well as a healthy number of studies
devoted specifically to the geography, phonology, grammar and
lexis of modern and historical dialects, and to literary dialect
and dialect literature.[9]

Comparative philology, however, was not inspired by Romanticism alone. Against a background of Positivism in philosophy and
science, and rapid progress in the natural sciences, it sought to apply
the methods of the latter to language[10] – which was often thought
of as an organism. An organism, of course, has both structure and
development, or history. Ellis's (1889) exercise in linguistic geography was intended to supply material for a fuller and more rigorous
understanding of the history of the English language. The shift
towards phonology was significant. Similarly, Wright's Windhill
monograph (1892) revealed a rigorous historical method, a concern
with phonology, and also some interest in morphology; his *English
Dialect Grammar* (1905) showed the same, although the lexical
component was still important. Indeed, the activities of the English
Dialect Society had been directed primarily towards the compilation
of *The English Dialect Dictionary*. Thus, the older interest in dialect
words had received something of a boost from Romanticism and
comparative philology. One need only compare a few entries from
The English Dialect Dictionary with entries in earlier dialect dictionaries to note a quite startling increase in systematicity, thoroughness
and historical scholarship: the layout of the entries, the supporting
quotations, the phonetics, the etymologies, etc.

Concern with sound change, and the regularity thereof, inspired not only the work of Wright, and the later monographs of the school of Wright,[11] but also gave an impetus to the development of linguistic geography. As we have noted already, Ellis began a geographical or descriptive survey for historical purposes. In continental Europe, dialect material was sought as a means of testing the Neogrammarian tenet that sound laws admit of no exceptions, *insofar as they proceed mechanically*. There is actually no proof in Wenker's writings that such a test was in his mind when he founded the *Deutscher Sprachatlas*,[12] but his successors demonstrated a keen interest in the question of the regularity or irregularity of sound change. Wenker himself simply said that he wanted to establish linguistic boundaries – a task that proved to be more complicated than he had expected.

Linguistic geography, or dialect geography, became the main direction in dialectology during the first half of the twentieth century. It provided comparable material that was of historical value, a means of evaluating the doctrine of the regularity of sound change, and information that might enable us to learn something about the nature of linguistic boundaries, and thereby to refine our notions of the very fuzzy concepts, *language* and *dialect*. At the same time, it produced data that are of interest in other disciplines such as anthropology, history, sociology, folklore, industrial archaeology and material culture – indeed, the history of civilization generally.[13] One cannot have a *Sprachatlas* that is not also a *Sachatlas*. I need hardly list here the many atlases that are the result of this particularly fruitful line in twentieth-century dialectology, both within the English-speaking world and without. Only with the advent of transformational-generative grammar and sociolinguistics did linguistic geography come to be seen, in some quarters, as rather sterile and at best of only peripheral interest.[14] The lack of historical acumen in such criticisms was noted by Malkiel (1984, 42), who complained of Petyt's (1980) failure to make it clear to readers that

the various techniques of selecting informants, interviewing, recording the utterances on maps or in lists, and so forth, for the continental scholars of the Golden Age of dialect geography involved, to be sure, not irrelevancies but hardly more than mere preliminaries, the grand strategy being to amass a huge and well-ordered congeries of material that could eventually be used for a lexis-based cultural history. Thus,

the built-in paradox remained that large-scale synchronic research
projects were launched with the prime purpose in mind of activating
our grasp of diachrony, as regards individual historical events, and, at
the highest level, the broad-gauged study of causation (etiology).

The much more recent *Atlas Linguarum Europae* is broadly
conceived in the same way, and seeks to address questions of
language contact, of language and culture across national and
linguistic boundaries, of dialect continua, of linguistic universals, of
language as a reflection of cultural and demographic movements –
in short, the history of civilization (Weijnen et al. 1975).

After Wright, the dialect monograph moved in two important
directions, particularly – in the case of British English dialects –
under the influence of German, Scandinavian and Swiss scholars.[15]
Firstly, the descriptive component increased at the expense of the
historical and, secondly, the use of representative informants became
usual. Fieldwork techniques improved, and detailed phonetic
transcription was undertaken. The linguistic importance of strictly
synchronic description was slow to impress itself on dialectologists – perhaps because a lot of dialectology was done in English
departments, whose concerns were often more literary and historical
than technically linguistic. Eventually, however, the impact of structuralism began to be felt in linguistic geography with such notions as
the *diasystem*,[16] and in the monograph with the synchronic studies
of Sivertsen (1960), Stursberg (1970), Viereck (1966) and Wölck
(1965).[17] A rigorous phonology (phonemics) was at last at hand.
Here, I think, was the opportunity to meet a need that McIntosh
(1961, 104–5) had identified: 'no evidence is more directly important
than that assembled in a set of adequate dialect descriptions.' Not
only linguistic geographers and historical dialectologists, but sociolinguists and transformational grammarians as well are dependent
upon such studies.[18]
However, just when the methodology of structuralism was at
long last percolating through into the study of British English
dialects, and when the informants of the type desired by McIntosh
(1961, 85–6) were still available, two new movements sprang
up: transformational-generative grammar and sociolinguistics. Both
revealed an unfortunate tendency to denigrate approaches other
than their own.[19] Linguistic geography survived, of course, although
for a time it came to be thought of as a rather peripheral activity,

as noted above. However, what was strangled was the *widespread* application of structuralist techniques to dialectology. Thus, what I believe to be one of the most desirable things in English dialectology never came about, namely a series of reasonably comprehensive, scientific, comparable and comprehensible monographs, written within the same broad structuralist framework, and published, over a period of say twenty to thirty years.

The stultifying influences of sociolinguistics and transformational grammar and its successor theories bear more detailed scrutiny. I shall begin with the former, which will only be treated briefly here, because I have dealt elsewhere in some detail with quite a number of the issues involved (Shorrocks 1985; 1998, 41–6). For instance, to claim, as Trudgill (1974, 4) did, that 'non-sociological' studies do not make a contribution to theory is simply to hijack the term *theory* (Shorrocks 1985, 48–9), and to take no account of the dialectologist's purpose.[20] The claim to be describing the speech of all or a majority of the population is also suspect: short interviews, questionnaires and reading passages will not elicit the most residual traditional vernacular after any consistent fashion; nor can descriptions be called 'complete' when a mere handful of variables is under discussion. Further, the field techniques associated with this particular methodology ensure that the descriptions will be partial in terms of linguistic levels of description: they are totally unsuited to the elicitation of syntax. Our methods and field techniques cannot be separated from our purposes: if we wish to investigate syntax, then we must proceed in an appropriate manner (see further Shorrocks 1996, 1997, 1998, 1999). Unfortunately, however, sociolinguists have discouraged work of what they call a 'non-sociological' type. No wonder that so many of them think that there are few significant syntactic differences between one dialect and another![21]

The chief problem with a transformational-generative grammar is that it will only handle a restricted set of data, and that there is then a tendency to disregard whatever lies outside of the scope of the particular 'theory'. Strang (1974, 62) remarked:

Its inherent weakness lies in the impossibility of checking the exhaustiveness of the rules; whole ranges of possible constructions may be overlooked. There is at present another weakness, not inherent, but accidental, in that decisions about acceptability are wrongly assumed to be clear-cut, and therefore are not investigated.

The latter point may be 'accidental', but it presents an enormous problem nevertheless – a problem that is far more acute for someone describing a non-standard variety (Shorrocks 1981, 54–5). The dialectologist will seldom have a comprehensive command of the dialect that he is setting out to describe: as an educated person, perhaps of a different social class or even nationality from the native speakers of that dialect, and very likely of a different age group if traditional vernacular is involved, he can hardly appeal to his own intuition. Equally, anyone who has tried asking informants to judge the acceptability of utterances knows how problematic that can be. There are really no substitutes for a respectable corpus of data in dialectology.

Strang's former point is, of course, one that has been made by others too. What Lakoff (1973, 3–4) said about grammars of 'little-known' or 'exotic' languages is also relevant to grammars of dialects:

> I should like to say that I do not think that theory construction and verification is the only or even the most important mode of doing linguistics. Theorising is more glamorous these days than doing careful descriptive work. I think that is unfortunate. Linguistic description is still an art, and is not likely to become a science for a long time to come. Unfortunately it is an art that has begun to die just at the time when it should be flourishing most. The reason is that it is still widely believed that linguistic description of little-known languages should be formal and should follow some particular theory. But it has become clear in the past decade that no linguistic theory is anywhere near adequate to deal with most facts. What is wrong with formal descriptions is that they only allow for those facts that happen to be able to be dealt with by the given formalism. At this time in history, any description of a language that adheres strictly to some formal theory will not describe most of what is in the language. Moreover, as formal theories become outmoded, as is happening at an ever-increasing rate, descriptions of exotic languages made on the basis of those theories become increasingly less useful. I think the time has come for a return to the tradition of informal descriptions of exotic languages, written whenever possible in clear prose rather than in formal rules, so that such descriptions will still be useful and informative when present theories are long forgotten.

McDavid argued in a similar vein within dialectology, noting succinctly: 'Explanations can wait; the data cannot' (1980, 355), which reminds us of how much of interest might perish unrecorded.

He also asserted his belief in what I will call *hard data*: 'They [the essays in the volume] show a prejudice toward data rather than toward theory; but a field worker is obligated to write down what the informant says, not what the informant thinks he intended to say . . .' (1980, 354). Of American dialectology, he wrote:

It is a data-oriented discipline, in a land teeming with unrecorded data. However fine the theoretical extrapolations one may wish to make, the dialectologist's first duty is to present the data in such a way that any reader can replicate the conclusions – or failing to replicate them, can show where the original statement went astray. However unfashionable this position may be at any given time, it is one in which the dialectologist can take comfort. For sooner or later the fashion will change, and data-oriented linguistics, like Sir Roger de Coverley's coat, will again be in style. (1980, 280)

I suspect that the fashion is indeed changing back, as McDavid predicted, although the cost has been considerable: 'Systematic treatments of English syntax are rare. A decade and a half of transformational rule-writing has produced nothing more waterproof than we had before; in fact, the transformationalist's disparagement of data has discouraged objective comparative work' (McDavid 1980, 168). Sampson (1980, 146–7) argued this latter point very forcibly:

This drawback in Chomskyan linguistics [that it trains students to see what the theory can handle and to overlook what it cannot] has often been aggravated by an intolerant attitude, on the part of members of this school, towards purely descriptive work. One might suppose that a group concerned to discover universal features of language would be delighted about the existence of other linguists who aim to describe various individual languages for their own sake, and that the 'universalists' would warmly encourage such people to continue their work: such a division of labour means that instead of having to do their own donkey-work out in the field, the 'universalists' get much of the data they need handed them on a plate. But the Chomskyans have not always seen matters in this light; members of the school have on occasion gone so far as to claim explicitly that purely descriptive linguistic work simply has no right to exist . . . By contrast with the situation in America before the rise to prominence of the Chomskyan school, during much of the 1960s and 1970s fieldwork on exotic languages has tended to become a dying art – with obvious adverse consequences for the search for universals. That search, in its relationship to purely descriptive linguistics, may be compared to the work of the theoreticians *vis-à-vis* that of the experimentalists in subjects like physics or chemistry. People who pursue those subjects are well aware that progress in them comes only from a healthy symbiosis between scholars of both categories.

It might be profitable at this juncture to take an example from English dialectology of the application of Chomskyan grammar to English syntax in what to me is an all-too-typical hard-data vacuum. Parker, Riley and Meyer (1988) examined the matter of case assignment to pronouns in co-ordinate constructions. They argued that the normal rules governing case assignment are suspended in co-ordinate constructions, the noun phrase dominating the co-ordinate construction forming a barrier to government and therefore to case assignment (1988, 214). They maintained that 'the use of unexpected case forms in coordinate constructions, a phenomenon typically associated with nonstandard varieties of English, is predictable from structural principles assumed in Chomsky's theories of government and barriers . . .' Further, they maintained that their investigations demonstrated 'the continued relevance of current syntactic and pragmatic theory to the study of language variation' (1988, 231). Parker, Riley and Meyer did not delimit the kind of English they were describing in any way: their approach was poly- or panlectal. Nor have their so-called data been drawn from any recognizable corpus; indeed, the sentences, which feature the ubiquitous John, would seem to have been adduced to support the particular line of argument. Thus we have variation between *John and I were having a hard time* and *John and me were having a hard time*, and so on. Whilst such illustrations might well be based upon observation, the observation is too superficial and restricted. Francis Bacon knew better in 1605, as the following quotation from *The Advancement of Learning* makes clear (1861, 186):

For knowledge drawn freshly, and in our view, out of particulars, knoweth the best way to particulars again; and it hath much greater life for practice when the discourse attendeth upon the example, than when the example attendeth upon the discourse. For this is no point of order, as it seemeth at first, but of substance; for when the example is the ground, being set down in a history at large, it is set down with all circumstances, which may sometimes control the discourse thereupon

made, and sometimes supply it as a very pattern for action; whereas
the examples alleged for the discourse' sake are cited succinctly, and
without particularity, and carry a servile aspect towards the discourse
which they are brought in to make good.

Data taken from my Bolton corpus reveal objective-case pronouns
in utterances such as:

> *Us three went* [. . .]
> *'im as come afooar were theer.*
> 'He who came before was there.'
> *Thee come here!*
> (Cf. subjective form *theaw* 'thou'. *Thee* is not a vocative here.)
> (Shorrocks 1999, 76–80)

These few examples – and many others might be adduced – are
enough to show that objective-case pronouns can occur other than
as objects or as constituents in co-ordinate noun phrases in subject
function. Furthermore, the Bolton examples are not in any sense
esoteric: they are widely representative of English dialects. Indeed,
popular English the world over uses objective-case pronouns other
than in object function or co-ordinate noun phrases, despite Parker,
Riley and Meyer's assertions to the contrary. Here are a few
examples from Canadian English:

> *Us journalists often feel the pressure.* (CBC radio)
> *Her with her nose in the air is likely to feel the back of my hand.*
> *Them that wants it can have it.*
> *Them two knew where it was.*

If, however, we turn our attention to the dialects of the South-
West of England and Newfoundland, we find evidence of case assignment being decided by stress. Whilst the matter is by no means
straightforward, we can certainly conclude from available data that
simple pronoun subjects appear at times in the so-called objective
case; that simple pronoun objects appear at times in the so-called
subjective case; and that stress is in some measure a determining
factor. Thus, Parker, Riley and Meyer's assertion, that 'objective
case pronouns never appear as the subject of a tensed clause unless
they appear in a coordinate construction' (1988, 214), is wrong, as is
also their rejection of such sentences as *They promised I that they*

would go (1988, 215–16). This is a perfectly respectable sentence in many parts of Newfoundland! Further, such are the differences between the South-Western dialects and others that any panlectal approach seems to me to be foredoomed to failure. At any rate, it is certain that theorizing on the basis of insufficient evidence is so foredoomed.[22]

It is unfortunate, then, that grammarians of the transformational-generative school and their successors have discouraged much-needed descriptive work – work which would, in fact, have led to the development and refinement of their own theories. It must be doubtful whether we have worked out yet all the categories that are needed to analyse spoken language. We really need the categories before we can hope to formalize them (Glinz 1965, 102). Highly developed sciences can work with a hypothetico-deductive method; less highly developed ones need a somewhat more inductive or data-orientated approach. In the study of the spoken language, it would be appropriate, as Ruoff (1973, 63–4) remarked, to direct our attention towards the form and function of utterances, whose acceptability is often only statistically ascertainable, whose grammaticality may often only be judged from context, and which seldom manifest themselves as 'sentences'.

I believe that linguists generally are now somewhat less impressed by transformational grammar and its successor theories, and that they are beginning once again to accept the importance of respectable data. I believe also that dialectology is – at least to some extent[23] – shaking off the sociolinguistic shackles, as, for example, dialect geography is revitalized by statistics and the computer, and a new interest in syntax becomes apparent (with a degree of stimulation from corpus linguistics). There are, of course, valuable insights to be gained from social dialectology: not least, the notion of *systematic heterogeneity*, the statistically established links between linguistic variables and extralinguistic factors, and the challenging of de Saussure's *synchronic–diachronic* distinction.[24] And there are no doubt those who feel that generative phonology has made a contribution to English dialectology. Overall, however, recent decades have been expensive: intolerant adherents of dominant paradigms have in some measure controlled university appointments, granting agencies and publishers. When this happens, approaches other than the dominant one(s) are sadly neglected. Also, our historiography is affected – for the worse.

In respect of the first of these two consequences, I have suggested above that much-needed descriptive work has been discouraged: there has been a dearth of detailed descriptive work except for that in sociolinguistic studies. Dialect syntax in particular has been neglected. This is a pity. In my Bolton study (1999), I found many aspects of syntax – quite a number of them never described before – which differed from standard syntax. For example, the dialect has a *four-term* system of affirmative and negative reaction signals; it has forms of the second person singular interrogative of auxiliary verbs hitherto unremarked anywhere; more extensive use of the definite article than might have been expected from previous studies; several grammatical features that are realized primarily as glottal stricture; a system of personal pronouns in which the subjective forms – probably as in most other dialects apart from those of the South-West of England – are well on their way to becoming clitics; etc.[25] It is inconceivable that this particular urban dialect should be unique in these respects. But opportunities were certainly lost, as informants born, schooled and raised before the First World War became increasingly scarce. And, of course, such syntactic findings depend upon a methodology very different from that of the sociolinguist or transformational grammarian. It is necessary to live in the area, to get to know one's informants, and to make extensive unscripted tape recordings if dialect grammar is to be adequately described (cf. Shorrocks 1996, 1997, 1999).

The second consequence, that our historiography is adversely affected, can perhaps be more easily remedied. We have some good works dealing with the history of dialectology – particularly Francis's *Dialectology* (1983), although this neglects the early history of the discipline, and entire areas such as literary dialect; but we have some poor and misleading works too, notably Petyt's *The Study of Dialect* (1980), which sees everything through the lens of the Labov–Trudgill approach. Thus, the past is not seen for what it was, but for what it was not. It is impossible to write a balanced and informative history of the discipline in this manner.[26] A particularly devastating critique of such biased history-writing is to be found in Malkiel's review article 'Revisionist dialectology and mainstream linguistics' (1984).[27]

It would also be appropriate to mention here a number of trends in English dialectology which are largely neglected in the more recent histories of the discipline: (1) the relatively small body of work on occupational dialects – although this might be substantially increased by a review of travel literature, folkloristic studies, work in material culture, and so on; (2) studies of dialect literature; (3) studies of non-standard speech in otherwise standard literature. The last area has attracted a degree of attention from serious students for over a hundred years now, although a fair proportion of the work is in German and other foreign languages – often in the form of dissertations – and is not at all well known in English-speaking countries. (4) The applied side of the discipline – for example, the educational implications of dialectology – is also typically neglected outside of sociolinguistics, sociology and pedagogy.[28] (5) For a review of attitudes towards dialects, a foray into the specialized writings of psycholinguists and social psychologists would be necessary.[29] (6) The study of local toponyms and personal names. Clearly sins of *omission* can be at least as great as those *com*mitted in the course of biased history-writing.

Certainly, the purposes of scholars studying dialect literature as (a) an aesthetic phenomenon, (b) a social phenomenon and (c) linguistic evidence are very different from those of, say, the generative phonologist; similarly, the scholar concerned with literary dialect as part of a novelist's stylistic repertoire will find the Labovian paradigm of some interest, but only a fraction of what he needs. Mace's (1989) study, for example, looks at literary dialect in terms of geographical and chronological setting; of the social standing of characters and their degree of education; of humour; of the psychological state of mind of a character; of the desire of an author such as Lawrence to offer a critique of established values and so-called civilization; and so on.

Conclusions

In this essay I have suggested that the theories, methods and field techniques involved in our researches cannot be seen in isolation from the frame of reference for a study, which will include, as a major determinant, the purpose(s) of the dialectologist. The review of the discipline presented here, whilst selective and in many other ways inadequate, is nonetheless sufficient to reveal a whole range of purposes and interests that have stimulated dialectological work. Scholars have been interested in examining the structure of current usage, the nature of linguistic change, older literary texts, settlement history, the nature of linguistic boundaries, the language of particular activities, socially conditioned variation, linguistic universals, the formal properties of languages, dialect literature, the stylistic potential of literary dialect, cultural influences, etc. Sometimes, different goals will involve a concentration on different linguistic levels of description. Sociolinguistic studies have often been phonological, whereas work in the history of civilization is often lexical and semantic. Where such a multiplicity of interests exists, it makes no sense to insist upon the superiority of the transformational or sociolinguistic approach. Not only are the latter theoretically and methodologically less unimpeachable than their supporters imagine, but, as has been indicated above, they both offer only *partial* descriptions of the linguistic data available. Even if one were to feel that these partial descriptions were superior in terms of their explanatory power, it would still be inappropriate to discourage the collection and analysis of other data by other means. Further, it is impossible to make comparisons between approaches where the goals are very different in nature. I know of no scale of values, to borrow Malkiel's term, that enables one to compare an exercise in generative phonology with a literary analysis; or a sociological study of phonological variables with an examination of the syntax of a dialect area, or a lexical study concerned with the history of civilization. There is, surely, room for many purposes in dialectology, and for many different approaches. We currently lack a history of English dialectology that is at once comprehensive and tolerant; that focuses on the concept *purpose*, and tries to see the past on its own terms, as well as in terms of later work. To reproach a stone with the fact that it is not a flower is an exercise in futility. A comprehensive history of the discipline is a large undertaking, admittedly – and one that will get no smaller, if put off. Perhaps a conference and a substantial volume of historiographical papers would be a useful first step. It would certainly help to clarify what we understand by *dialectology*.

Notes

1 The frame of reference is impressionistic, and low on explicitness, but becomes a theory as it is made explicit (Verhaar 1970, 42). Cf. Chao (1970, 16), with the provisos noted in Shorrocks (1981, 31, footnote 5). *Theory* can further be defined as 'a certain method justified', where

method is 'the actual manner of pursuing research' (Verhaar 1970, 42), 'the ways and means by which the things are to be studied in order to arrive at a theory about them' (Chao 1970, 15). There is a sense in which method justifies and evaluates theory, so that the definitions of *theory* and *method* are interdependent, or circular. *Hypothesis* belongs 'to method rather than theory, by reason of its largely provisional and operational character' (Verhaar 1970, 43). Malkiel's (1984, 30–1) remarks about extralinguistic influences on what constitutes 'mainstream linguistics' are of interest here.

2 For an illustration of purpose as part of the frame of reference for a study, see Shorrocks (1981, 32–3). Extralinguistic factors were also part of the frame of reference (1981, 28, 32–3, 76–7, 681).

3 Nowell's work, probably written between 1561 and 1566, is a manuscript dictionary of Old English. Where possible, he illustrated his entries with surviving dialectal words – 173 from his native Lancashire, and seventeen from elsewhere. See further Marckwardt (1947, 1952).

4 The first edition appeared in 1746. The most useful edition for scholars is probably Fishwick (1894).

5 Edmund Coote, *The English Schoole-Master* (1597). Cited after Wakelin (1994, 37–8).

6 *Gentleman's Magazine*, 16 (1746), 527. It is generally thought that this 'dry and unentertaining' piece passed through some sixty editions, many of them pirated. Tomlinson (1966), however, listed 104 editions (not all of them located), and unpublished investigations by Paul Smith and myself have uncovered yet more.

7 Cf. Kluckhohn (1966, 113–14). This same work contains useful sections on history, the sense of national identity, and other key notions.

8 Cf., for example, Storm (1896). Storm wrote: 'Als die Tendenzen der gebildeten Sprache vielfach bestimmend und als die Keim der Zukunft oft in sich tragend, ist auch die Volkssprache sehr zu beachten' (p.772) ('Folk speech is particularly worthy of attention in that it determines the tendencies of educated language in many ways and carries the seeds of the future in itself' (my translation)).

9 Whilst articles and monographs of a more 'linguistic' character can be found in the usual bibliographies, there is no satisfactory listing of works dealing with either literary dialect or dialect literature. (I am currently working on bibliographies in these areas.)

10 Cf., for example, Schleicher (1983 [1850]), and Koerner's introductory essay to this reprint.

11 I think, too, that there is the epistemological question of how one arranges data. Before the concept of a synchronic system became established, arrangement of data within a historical framework probably seemed quite natural.

12 Published as Wrede, Martin and Mitzka (1927–56). Wrede saw the *Sprachatlas* as a test of the Neogrammarian tenet.
13 Wakelin (1994, 10) observed:

> [T]raditional linguistic geography has always found it necessary to concern itself with 'external' phenomena – external, that is, to purely linguistic matters – since it conceives part of the task to be the relating of dialect features to geographical, historical, social, political and other factors.

The insights that language can offer into settlement history have been of major concern, as have specific problems in historical linguistics. For instance, Wright and Wright (1923, 2–3) noted that we would never establish Middle English dialect boundaries properly until we had a good atlas of present-day dialects. See also Frings (1922) on the relationship between linguistic and extralinguistic factors, and Malkiel (1984, 60, footnote 6) on the link between traditional approaches to dialectology and other disciplines.

14 Cf. Francis (1983, vii), who felt that dialectology was by then starting to move back into the area of central interest.
15 Dieth (1946, 80–2) listed the monographs on dialects of British English written up to 1942, and drew attention to the small contribution of Englishmen. Dieth's listing was incomplete, however. See also the much less well-known article by Schubel (1939).
16 Cf. Weinreich (1954). There is a useful discussion of structural dialect geography in Francis (1983, 158–71). The Linguistic Survey of Scotland was, of course, particularly influenced by structuralism.
17 These four studies are limited to the phonological level – the level at which structuralist techniques are best developed.
18 The usefulness of 'traditional' syntactic description to transformational-generative grammar is commented upon extensively, below. See in particular the quotation from Sampson (1980, 146–7). Similarly, socio-linguists are dependent upon the much-despised 'traditional' description. McDavid (1980, 211) commented:

> As different as are the interests of William Labov from those of the Atlas, he admits his study of New York City speech would have been impossible without the records which Lowman made in 1940–41. The study of dialects, like any other study of human behaviour, is cumulative and continuing, with each investigation building on its predecessors.

Similarly (1980, 209–10):

> [A] first-stage general survey of a wide area is bound to stress the older and more stable elements in the population, and the more

traditional elements in the language system. To young Turks, impatient to grapple with the language problems of seething urban multitudes, such an emphasis may seem quaint or 'ruralistic', but it is necessary background for their investigations – and of course it has its uses in other kinds of linguistic work, notably in reconstructing the past stages of the language.

19 Some evidence to support this assertion is contained in the present study. See also Shorrocks (1985), which cites a number of observations by sociolinguists, and Shorrocks (1983; 1998, 41ff.; 1999, 18–20).

20 Malkiel (1984, 49) drew attention to Petyt's (1980, 135) assumption that settlement history is somehow inferior in itself to insights into present-day social structure. See further the points cited in note 27 below.

21 The view is, of course, by no means confined to sociolinguists. A representative reiteration of the traditional – in my view erroneous – wisdom is Wakelin (1984, 84): 'Dialectal syntactical constructions often parallel those of Standard English, with only few exceptions, as far as is known.' A dissenting voice is that of Lodge (1979, 169): 'That both standard and non-standard varieties of English have a lot in common is not in dispute (otherwise it would be difficult to call them both English), but the differences between them are considerably greater than one might expect.' I have discussed the matter in greater detail elsewhere (Shorrocks 1981, 493–6; 1999, 15–21).

22 For a fuller discussion of Parker, Riley and Meyer's article, see Shorrocks (1992). My position in this matter is supported by Denison (1996, 294–5).

23 A hard-line note is sometimes evident. For instance, Edwards (1986, 48) made the quite astonishing remark that 'the study of British dialects has until quite recently been rather pedestrian'. Quite to the contrary, I find the work of the nineteenth-century figures, Ellis and Wright, to be both innovative and stimulating. See, for instance, Shorrocks (1991 and in press) on the achievements of Ellis and Wright. Cf. further in this connection Malkiel's (1984, 29) observation that a bright student might think social dialectology dull, since its practitioners are so sure of how everything should be done; and his conclusion (1984, 59–60): 'The scope of urban dialectology is, upon reflection, scarcely wide enough to keep truly brilliant scholars excited, for many years in succession, with it as their dominant or exclusive focus of intellectual curiosity.'

24 Cf. Sampson (1980, 129):

> Often, what a given speaker perceives as a difference between more or less socially prestigious styles of speech will coincide historically with a difference between newer and older usage, as speakers in each generation unconsciously modify their speech slightly in order to raise their social prestige.

And further:

> The Prague School and, now, Labov are amongst the linguists who
> have taken the social dimension of language most seriously; and they
> have ended by destroying Saussure's sharp separation between
> synchronic and diachronic study. For the individual, it turns out, a
> sizeable portion of the history of the language *is* psychologically real;
> only he perceives it not as history but as social stratification.

25 See further Shorrocks (1999) and the references cited there.
26 The whole idea of positive development, of one approach *building* on
   another, is missing in this kind of historiography – cf. the dependence
   of sociolinguistics and transformational grammar on more conventional work, discussed above.
27 Malkiel rightly complained about Petyt's being 'infatuated with this
   single standard of excellence' (1984, 50–1), and about the concomitant
   disparagement of other approaches (1984, 60, footnotes 1 and 2).
   He asked (1984, 30) of Petyt (1980) and Chambers and Trudgill (1980):
   'On what serious criteria do they base the validity of their scale(s) of
   values in, again and again, placing phonology above the gamut of
   lexicological disciplines (including the etymological bugaboo)?' Further,
   he complained in respect of Petyt (1980) about specific cases involving
   'serious distortions' (1984, 44), and about the confusion and misrepre-
   sentation involved in lumping the various 'traditional' approaches
   together and making them into one (1984, 46). He concluded: 'Not once
   does the author take up the cudgels in defence of dialect study, even
   at its most advanced, against external criticism. The surrender to
   sociology is unconditional (and, of course, both unrealistic and somehow unsavoury)' (1984, 47). Penhallurick (1992) effectively took up the
   question of treating the various 'traditional' approaches as one. See also
   Shorrocks (1983).
28 Trudgill (1984) addresses various issues in applied sociolinguistics.
29 See, for example, Ryan and Giles (1982). A useful collection of articles
   is to be found in Greenbaum (1985).

Works cited

Bacon, Francis. 1861 [1605]. *The Advancement of Learning*. Edited by G. W.
   Kitchin. London: J. M. Dent and Sons. Distributed by Heron Books.
Chambers, J. K. and Peter Trudgill. 1980. *Dialectology*. Cambridge: Cam-
   bridge University Press. 2nd edition 1998.
Chao, Y.-R. 1970. Some aspects of the relation between theory and method.
   In P. L. Garvin (ed.), *Method and Theory in Linguistics* (Janua Linguarum,
   Series Maior, 40), pp.15–26. The Hague and Paris: Mouton, 1970.

Collier, John [pseudonym Tim Bobbin]. [1746]. *A View of the Lancashire Dialect*. Manchester.

——. 1746. Vocabulary of the Lancashire dialect. *Gentleman's Magazine*, 16 (1746), 527–8.

Coote, Edmund. 1597. *The English Schoole-Master*. London.

Delbrück, Berthold. 1989 (1974). *Introduction to the Study of the History and Methods of Comparative Philology of Indo-European Languages* (Amsterdam Studies in the Theory and History of Linguistic Science, Series I, Amsterdam Classics in Linguistics, 1800-1925, volume 8). New edition with a Foreword and Selected Bibliography by Konrad Koerner. [An 1882 translation of the first edition (1880) of the work.] Amsterdam and Philadelphia: John Benjamins.

Denison, David. 1996. The case of the unmarked pronoun. In Derek Britton (ed.), *English Historical Linguistics 1994. Papers from the 8th International Conference on English Historical Linguistics* (8. ICEHL, Edinburgh, 19–23 September 1994), pp.287–99. (Amsterdam Studies in the Theory and History of Linguistic Science, Series IV, Current Issues in Linguistic Theory, 135.) Amsterdam and Philadelphia: John Benjamins.

Dieth, Eugen. 1946. A new survey of English dialects. *Essays and Studies by Members of the English Association*, 32, pp.74–104. Oxford: Clarendon, 1947.

Edwards, Viv. 1986. Dialectics. *Transactions of the Yorkshire Dialect Society*, part 86, volume 16 (1986), 48–51. Reprinted from the *Times Educational Supplement*, 2 May 1986.

Ellis, Alexander John. 1889. *On Early English Pronunciation*. Part V. *The Existing Phonology of English Dialects Compared with that of West Saxon Speech*. London: Early English Text Society.

Fishwick, Henry. 1894. *The Works of John Collier (Tim Bobbin) in Prose and Verse*. Rochdale: James Clegg, Aldine Press.

Francis, W. N. 1983. *Dialectology: An Introduction*. London and New York: Longman.

Frings, Theodor. 1922. *Sprache und Geschichte*. Halle (Saale).

Gaskell, Elizabeth. 1848. *Mary Barton: A Tale of Manchester Life*. Two volumes. London: Chapman and Hall.

Gaskell, William. 1854. *Two Lectures on the Lancashire Dialect*. London: Chapman and Hall.

Glinz, Hans. 1965. *Deutsche Syntax*. Sammlung Metzler. Stuttgart: Metzlersche Verlagsbuchhandlung. 2nd edition 1967.

Greenbaum, Sidney (ed.). 1985. *The English Language Today*. Oxford: Pergamon Institute of English.

Halliwell, James Orchard. 1847. *Dictionary of Archaic and Provincial Words*. London: Russell Smith.

Kluckhohn, Paul. 1966. *Das Ideengut der deutschen Romantik*. 5th edition. Tübingen: Niemeyer.

Lakoff, George. 1973. *Interview with Herman Parrett*. Reproduced by Linguistic Agency, University of Trier, D-55, Trier.

Levitt, John. 1989. Dialect study then and now. *Journal of the Lancashire Dialect Society*, 38 (1989), 7–16.

Lodge, K. R. 1979. A three-dimensional analysis of non-standard English. *Journal of Pragmatics*, 3 (1979), 169–95.

McDavid, Raven I., Jr. 1980. *Varieties of American English: Essays by Raven I. McDavid, Jr*. Selected and introduced by Anwar S. Dil. Stanford: Stanford University Press.

Mace, Renate. 1989. *Funktionen des Dialekts im regionalen Roman von Gaskell bis Lawrence*. Tübingen: Gunter Narr.

McIntosh, Angus. 1961. *An Introduction to a Survey of Scottish Dialects*. Edinburgh: T. Nelson for the University of Edinburgh.

Malkiel, Jakov. 1984. Revisionist dialectology and mainstream linguistics (review article). *Language in Society*, 13 (1984), 29–66.

Marckwardt, Albert H. 1947. An unnoted source of English dialect vocabulary. *Journal of English and Germanic Philology*, 46 (1947), 177–82.

——. 1952. *Laurence Nowell's 'Vocabularium Saxonicum'*. Ann Arbor: University of Michigan Press; London: Geoffrey Cumberlege, Oxford University Press.

Parker, Frank, Kathryn Riley and Charles Meyer. 1988. Case assignment and the ordering of constituents in coordinate constructions. *American Speech*, 63 (1988), 214–33.

Penhallurick, Robert. 1992. The politics of dialectology. *Lore and Language*, 9, 2 (1990, but published 1992), 55–68.

Petyt, K. M. 1980. *The Study of Dialect: An Introduction to Dialectology*. London: André Deutsch.

Ruoff, Arno. 1973. *Grundlagen und Methoden der Untersuchung gesprochener Sprache*. Tübingen: Max Niemeyer Verlag.

Ryan, Ellen Bouchard and Howard Giles (eds.). 1982. *Attitudes towards Language Variation: Social and Applied Contexts*. London: Edward Arnold.

Sampson, Geoffrey. 1980. *Schools of Linguistics: Competition and Evolution*. London: Hutchinson.

Schleicher, August. 1983 [1850]. *Die Sprachen Europas in systematischer Übersicht. Linguistische Untersuchungen* (Amsterdam Studies in the Theory and History of Linguistic Science, Series I, Amsterdam Classics in Linguistics, 1800–1925, volume 4). New edition, with a preface and introductory article by Konrad Koerner. Amsterdam and Philadelphia: John Benjamins.

Schubel, Friedrich. 1939. Zur neueren englischen Dialektforschung. *Englische Studien*, 73 (1938/39), 344–80.

Shorrocks, Graham. 1981. *A Grammar of the Dialect of Farnworth and District (Greater Manchester County, Formerly Lancashire)*. Ph.D. thesis, University of Sheffield, 1980. Published by University Microfilms International, xerographic form and microform, number 81-70, 023.

——. 1983. Review of K. M. Petyt, *The Study of Dialect: An Introduction to Dialectology. Journal of the Lancashire Dialect Society*, 32 (1983), 32–4.

——. 1985. Further thoughts on the Labovian interview. *Lore and Language*, 4, 1 (1985), 46–56.

——. 1991. Ellis as dialectologist: a reassessment. *Historiographia Linguistica*, 18/2–3 (1991), 321–34.

——. 1992. Case assignment in simple and coordinate constructions in present-day English. *American Speech*, 67/4 (1992), 432–44.

——. 1996. The second person singular interrogative in the traditional vernacular of the Bolton metropolitan area. In James Black and Virginia Motapanyane (eds.), *Microparametric Syntax: Dialect Variation in Syntax*. Selected, refereed papers from the 1994 Atlantic Provinces Linguistic Association's Conference. Two volumes. (Current Issues in Linguistic Theory, 77), pp.169–88. Amsterdam and Philadelphia: John Benjamins.

——. 1997. Field methods and non-standard grammar. In Heinrich Ramisch and Kenneth Wynne (eds.), *Language in Time and Space: Studies in Honour of Wolfgang Viereck on the Occasion of his 60th Birthday* (*Zeitschrift für Dialektologie und Linguistik*, Beiheft 97), pp.212–22. Stuttgart: Franz Steiner Verlag.

——. 1998. *A Grammar of the Dialect of the Bolton Area. Part I. Introduction, Phonology*. (Bamberger Beiträge zur Englischen Sprachwissenschaft, volume 41.) Frankfurt am Main: Peter Lang.

——. 1999. *A Grammar of the Dialect of the Bolton Area. Part II. Morphology and Syntax*. (Bamberger Beiträge zur Englischen Sprachwissenschaft, volume 42.) Frankfurt am Main: Peter Lang.

——. In press. The dialectology of English in the British Isles. In Sylvain Auroux et al. (eds.), *Geschichte der Sprachwissenschaften/History of the Language Sciences/Histoire des sciences du langage: An International Handbook on the Evolution of the Study of Languages from the Beginnings to the Present*. (Handbooks of Linguistics and Communication Science.) Berlin and New York: Walter de Gruyter.

Sivertsen, E. 1960. *Cockney Phonology*. Oslo: Oslo University Press.

Storm, Johan. 1896. *Englische Philologie. Anleitung zum wissenschaftlichen Studium der englischen Sprache*. 2nd edition, two volumes. Leipzig: O. R. Reisland.

Strang, Barbara M. H. 1974. *A History of English*. London: Methuen.

Stursberg, Mario. 1970. *The Stressed Vowels in the Dialects of Longtown, Abbey Town, and Hunsonby (Cumberland): A Structural Approach*. Basel: Econom-Druck.

Tomlinson, Victor I. 1966. Tummus and Tim: a handlist of editions of John Collier's *View of the Lancashire Dialect*. Unpublished list prepared to illustrate a paper read to a joint meeting of the Lancashire Dialect Society and the Manchester Bibliographical Society (9 February 1966, Salford).

Trudgill, Peter. 1974. *The Social Differentiation of English in Norwich*. Cambridge: Cambridge University Press.

—— (ed.). 1984. *Applied Sociolinguistics*. London: Academic Press.

Verhaar, J. W. M. 1970. Method, theory and phenomenology. In P. L. Garvin (ed.), *Method and Theory in Linguistics* (Janua Linguarum, Series Maior, 40), pp.42–91. The Hague and Paris: Mouton.

Viereck, Wolfgang. 1966. *Phonematische Analyse des Dialekts von Gateshead-upon-Tyne/Co. Durham*. Hamburg: Cram, de Gruyter & Co.

Wakelin, Martyn F. 1984. Rural dialects in England. In Peter Trudgill (ed.), *Language in the British Isles*, pp.70–93. Cambridge: Cambridge University Press.

——. 1994. *English Dialects: An Introduction*. Reprint of the revised [2nd] edition of 1977. London: Athlone Press.

Weijnen, A. et al. (eds.). 1975. *Atlas Linguarum Europae (ALE). Introduction*. Assen: van Gorcum.

Weinreich, Uriel. 1954. Is a structural dialectology possible? *Word*, 10 (1954), 388–400.

Whitehall, Harold. 1933. Thomas Shadwell and the Lancashire dialect. *Michigan University Publications, Language and Literature, Studies in English and Comparative Literature*, 10 (1933), 261–78.

Wölck, W. 1965. *Phonematische Analyse der Sprache von Buchan* (Frankfurter Arbeiten aus dem Gebiete der Anglistik und der Amerika-Studien, 10). Heidelberg: Carl Winter.

Wrede, Ferdinand, B. Martin and W. Mitzka (eds.). 1927–56. *Deutscher Sprachatlas*. Marburg: Elwert.

Wright, Joseph. 1892. *A Grammar of the Dialect of Windhill in the West Riding of Yorkshire* (EDS, 67). London: Kegan Paul, Trench, Trübner & Co. for the English Dialect Society.

—— (ed.). 1898–1905. *The English Dialect Dictionary*. Six volumes. Oxford: Frowde.

——. 1905. *The English Dialect Grammar*. Oxford: Henry Frowde. Also published in volume 6 of Wright 1898–1905.

—— and Elizabeth Mary Wright. 1923. *An Elementary Middle English Grammar*. London: Humphrey Milford, Oxford University Press.

Wright, Thomas. 1857. *Dictionary of Obsolete and Provincial English*. [Bohn's Reference Library.] Two volumes. London: Henry G. Bohn. Another edition: two volumes, George Bell and Sons, 1880. Republished Detroit: Gale Research Company, 1967.

5

Theory, Objectivity and the Discipline: Further Discussion

ROBERT PENHALLURICK AND
GRAHAM SHORROCKS

Robert Penhallurick

Dear Graham, How easily do you think the adjectives *objective* and *scientific* rest with *linguistics* or, more specifically, with *dialectology*? You quite properly question that expression of common consent, *scientific linguistics*, suggesting that linguistics is still an art, but also that, through the appropriate inductive approaches, the prized label *science* is attainable. Is it? – if we are dealing with 'the history of civilization', and when the character of the linguistic 'fact' is so indeterminate? What if the only way in which linguistics, or dialectology, can become 'scientific' is through the kind of reductive approach, such as the transformational-generative approach, which you criticize? This of course either amounts to no science or to pseudo-science, unless one believes that it is the nature of all science to be reductive.

When the study of spoken English not only touches on but incorporates and is incorporated in so much of human life, is 'science' even desirable? Taking this and another line of your argument further, whereby we end up with a data-collecting discipline which is not restricted by *theory*, do we then have a *discipline* at all? Do we want one, do we need one? Except that *theory* is not so easily disposed of. Because of the conventions of linguistics it is tempting to distinguish 'theoretical' linguistics from other kinds, but, and allowing for your teasing out of terminological strands, I am not sure that data-orientated historical dialectology is any less 'theoretical' than transformational-generative linguistics. To believe in 'hard data' is to assume a deeply theoretical position – although I may now have strayed from your closely confined definition of *theory*, which probably would not permit the term to be likened to others such as *belief* or *world-view*.

Whenever *objective* is used in linguistics (or anywhere else, I suppose) my reaction is often, in part at least, suspicion. Is your use of the term tactical, that is, indicating an intention to redress the balance in the historiography of dialectology? If not, who will write the 'objective history'? Do we not all tend 'to denigrate approaches other than [our] own'? Can we ever see 'the past on its own terms'?

One more point: those who took part in the quarrel between 'traditional' and 'sociolinguistic' dialectology sometimes euphemistically talked of differences in approach, although it was goals as well as methods that were under attack, in other words, not a case of reproaching a stone with the fact that it is not a flower but saying that we should forget about the stone altogether.

Graham Shorrocks

Let me begin with your questions about the term *objective*. I take it to be axiomatic, that there is no knowledge without a perceiving subject. Thus, knowledge cannot be absolute, nor can we hope for absolute objectivity. However, the fact that one cannot know things absolutely does not mean that rigorous thinking and relative objectivity therefore fly out of the window. We can certainly have our conceptions of the past, and my plea here is for ones which take context, including (likely) purposes, into account. Note that I asked for historiography that '*tries* to see the past on its own terms' (emphasis added), and that the adjectival *objective* in my subtitle is preceded by a qualifier.

How appropriate are terms such as *scientific* to linguistics/dialectology, and am I not, perhaps, contradicting myself by citing Lakoff, who calls linguistic description an *art*, with obvious approval on one occasion and using the term *scientific* on another? Well, medicine is certainly both a science and an art at one and the same time – there is no contradiction in that. In my reference to the 'common consent', whereby a scientific linguistics 'did not begin until the nineteenth century', the key word is *begin*. I do not see linguistics (and therefore also dialectology) as being either a science or an art *in all respects* and *for all time*. But I do think that the discipline is in certain respects more scientific than it was, and that it will, with time, move further along the road towards the scientific status that it craves so ardently. The 'common consent' is, I believe, quite correct in respect of such matters as the nineteenth-century advances in phonetics, and some aspects of linguistic taxonomy, typology and historical-comparative method; and in respect of the 'objectivity' inherent in the process of *discovery*, whereby we now 'know' things that we previously did not. That does not mean, however, that synchronic syntax is now a hard science. Nor, equally, is Lakoff saying that scientific status is unattainable – merely that it is a long way off. Scientific status is not an all-or-nothing affair, but rather a question of degree. And, no, a hypothetico-deductive method is not the only way to do science – instrumental phonetics would score very highly by such criteria as objectivity and replicability.

Further to my use of the terms *science* and *scientific*, I would say that science is not a hard-and-fast concept. It is a tradition – an evolving tradition of critical inquiry. It perhaps began in western culture with people like Socrates asking critically for reasons other than appeals to authority. Because science is an evolving tradition, it is difficult – if not, ultimately, impossible – to crystallize the method at any given moment. Science is a search for truth, even if, as I indicated earlier, that truth is not ascertainable in absolute terms; and it is a disciplined dynamic search, with method.

It is, of course, true, that some disciplines deal with 'objects' that are less tractable than others. As you note, the study of spoken English is so complex that it can be extremely difficult, and at times impossible, to control for variables. Again, though, this does not mean that we toss strict thinking overboard, and abandon the terms *theory* and *discipline*. I think that we do need them – at least if *theory* is understood as I have defined it here, and if the pronouncements of linguists are to be distinguishable from those of the tabloid press. I should like, if I may, to quote something which I wrote earlier (1981, 221) (see p.106) about the scientific status of dialectological work and which is relevant here, though I withdraw the word 'slightly':

An important criterion of scientific status is that data be open to inspection, or checking. The availability of data for checking, along with biographical and other contextual data, and together with explicit statements concerning the setting up and conduct of an experiment, determines the repeatability of that experiment. *Repeatability* is an essential determinant of scientific status. Ultimately, particular data obtained from particular informants under circumstances x, y and z are unrepeatable: the fieldwork is a creative and subjective process, which cannot be specified in all its aspects. The transcription process too has been shown to be somewhat subjective. Yet these facts do not invalidate the quest for a rigorous use of scientific method any more than the observation that no two snowflakes are alike invalidates the concept *snowflake*. The issue is one of degree, and the search for scientific status in linguistic work should not be abandoned simply because human beings provide slightly less hard data than, say, rocks. Consequently, it is an especial requirement on dialect studies, that an honest and thorough account be offered of all aspects of data gathering and data processing. Where problems or omissions are evident to the dialectologist in his work they should be explicitly stated.

Incidentally, I should not care to equate *theory* with *Weltanschauung* (*world-view*). The latter is part of the *frame of reference* and has much to do with *purpose*. It bears on *theory*, but is not coterminous with it.

Finally, I think we are in agreement that it is indeed goals or purposes that have often been under attack: I believe this is evident in my insistence on the link between theory and method on the one hand and purpose on the other; and on the fact that it is not possible to rank studies written to radically different ends. However, the debate has certainly often been couched in other terms.

6

Dialectology and Deconstruction

NICHOLAS ROYLE

> The accused is thus someone who re-establishes contact between the corpora and the ceremonies of several dialects. (*L'accusé, c'est donc celui qui remet en contact les corps et les cérémonies de plusieurs dialectes.*)

This is Jacques Derrida, in an interview in 1983, defending himself as a writer who is accused of being 'unreadable'. The statement goes on: 'If he or she is a philosopher, then it's because he or she speaks neither in a purely academic milieu, with the language, rhetoric, and customs that are in force there, nor in that "language of everyone" which we all know does not exist' (Derrida 1983a, 116). In a perhaps unexpected fashion, Derrida's conception of the writer or philosopher is here phrased in terms of 'corpora' and 'dialects'. To many there may appear to be nothing short of an abyss between dialectology and deconstruction. I would like to suggest, however, that there are significant correspondences between them, and that in a certain sense it is ultimately perhaps not possible to think about the future of the one without the other. What follows is highly provisional and preliminary, confining itself simply to four brief remarks.

(1) The dialectologist is a writer. This proposition has perhaps not received the attention its self-evident truth might encourage one to expect. The formulation from Derrida cited above is especially provoking in this context: like the philosopher, the dialectologist could be described as 'someone who re-establishes contact between the corpora and the ceremonies of several dialects'. Like the philosopher, the dialectologist works with language, across and between languages, in a language which is neither one thing nor the other (neither 'purely academic' nor 'that "language of everyone" which we all know does not exist'). And in the midst of all this accounting and theorization of speech, above all like the

philosopher, the dialectologist *writes*. At least in principle then, one might suppose dialectology, like philosophy, to be especially attuned to the decisive, indeed founding importance of the concept, event and trace of *writing* within it.[1] A sustained meditation on this question would accompany, inflect and perhaps transform any rigorous attempt to provide the comprehensive history of the discipline of dialectology for which Graham Shorrocks calls in the present volume. No history or account of dialectology is possible without reckoning with the strangely, perhaps exemplarily 'philosophical' character of dialectology as a discipline for which there cannot be a proper language (only a jamming and production involving 'several dialects', always more than two dialects, and every one of them differently 'proper' *and* 'improper' at the same time), as a discipline whose ostensible concern with the (non-existent) 'language of everyone' is indissociably bound up with a history, theory and politics of writing, not least with the account of itself *as* written archive.

(2) The dialectologist, perhaps, does not exist. Such a suggestion may sound faintly scandalous or absurd, but there is a curious homology in this context between the dialectologist and the deconstructionist. Just as it has been argued that there cannot be a subject *of* deconstruction,[2] an agent or practitioner who is not subject *to* deconstruction, so one is perhaps obliged to reckon with the notion that there cannot be a subject *of* dialectology. If there is a future for dialectology, and if there is a future for deconstruction, it may be that this will entail the elaboration of discursive and political possibilities that are reducible neither to 'science' (as though the only true dialectologist would be somehow purely detached, objective, fundamentally not responsible for or even implicated in the products and production of dialectology) nor to 'fiction' (as though the dialectologist were the linguistic impresario, producing what is an admittedly fabricated account in ways that ultimately can be ascribed to his or her mastery over language, information and tradition, bearing witness to the unique character of his or her intervention in the field). Like deconstruction, in this regard, dialectology might be figured or refigured as 'the opening of the future itself' (see Derrida 1992, 200). Far from seeing dialectology as an outmoded or dying discipline, one might see it as on the eve of another beginning, a quite different articulation and elaboration.

(3) In some respects, after all, deconstruction *is* dialectology. Contrary to what some may have supposed, Derrida's work is

not 'anti-voice', nor is it primarily concerned simply with a reversal (if such a thing were even possible) of the perceived hierarchies of speech/writing and a consequent privileging of 'writing' over 'speech'. Rather, it can increasingly be seen that his most intimate concern is with speech and with the experience of voice. As he emphasizes in the interview entitled 'Unsealing ("the old new language")', Derrida has written numerous books with 'several voices' (Derrida 1983a, 130), experimenting with dialogue and with the overflowing of dialogue form, a polyphonic tracery. All of Derrida's work could in fact be described as a kind of dialectology, as a preoccupation with the idea of doing justice to different voices, different kinds of speech, with the idea of an affirmative difference *within* voice, with what at once conditions and exceeds the singularity of a voice or of a dialect which may be peculiar to a subject, district or country.[3] To recall one of Derrida's most succinct definitions, deconstruction is *'plus d'une langue'* – both 'more than a language and no more of *a* language' (Derrida 1986, 15). As he has put it in a recent extraordinary essay on monolingualism: 'No such thing as *a* language exists. At present. Nor does the language. Nor the idiom or dialect' (Derrida 1998, 65). *Plus d'une langue*: might this not be an apt password for dialectology as well?

(4) If, after dialectology, the name of the discipline were to be preserved (as with every 'after-word' or after-formation), still it would perhaps be necessary to invent other names, to inaugurate different terms and different kinds of concepts to mark what, after all, is implied by the allusion to the abyss with which we began, namely a revolution and transformation of what has happened under the aegis of 'dialectology' to date. Such terms and concepts might include, for example, 'dialectronics' or 'spectrolinguistics', as possible names for trying to elaborate ways in which the electronic Derridean epoch has altered and continues to alter conceptions of identity, voice, time and place. The future belongs to ghosts, as Derrida has observed, and 'modern image technology, cinema, telecommunications, etc., are only increasing the power of ghosts' (Derrida and Bennington 1993, 349). Dialectology shares with deconstruction a love of memory and the archive, a respect for the strangeness of remains, margins and the idiomatic; it has also, from the beginning, been a discipline attentive to the voices of the dead, a responsiveness to the ghostly character of the present and of itself.

Notes

1 For an extended account of the notion of the trace and for the argument that 'writing opens the field of history' (p.27), see Derrida (1976).
2 See, for example, Readings (1989).
3 For some sense of the variety of Derrida's attention to questions of voice, speech and difference, see, for example, Derrida (1982, 1983b, 1984a, 1984b, 1998).

Works cited

Derrida, Jacques. 1976. *Of Grammatology*. Trans. Gayatri Spivak. Baltimore: Johns Hopkins University Press.

——. 1982. Qual quelle: Valéry's sources. In *Margins of Philosophy*, trans. Alan Bass, pp.273–306. Chicago: University of Chicago Press.

——. 1983a. Unsealing ('the old new language'). Trans. Peggy Kamuf, in *Points . . . Interviews, 1974–1994*, ed. Elisabeth Weber, trans. Peggy Kamuf and others, pp.115–31. Stanford: Stanford University Press, 1995. (For the original French text see Desceller ('la vieille neuve langue'). In *Points de suspension: Entretiens*, choisis et présentés par Elisabeth Weber, pp.123–40. Paris: Galilée, 1992.)

——. 1983b. 'Dialanguages'. Trans. Peggy Kamuf, in *Points . . . Interviews, 1974–1994*, ed. Elisabeth Weber, trans. Peggy Kamuf and others, pp.132–55. Stanford: Stanford University Press, 1995.

——. 1984a. Of an apocalyptic tone recently adopted in philosophy. Trans. John P. Leavey, Jr. *Oxford Literary Review*, 6, 2 (1984), 3–37.

——. 1984b. Voice II. Trans. Verena Conley, in *Points . . . Interviews, 1974–1994*, ed. Elisabeth Weber, trans. Peggy Kamuf and others, pp.156–70. Stanford: Stanford University Press, 1995.

——. 1986. *Mémoires: For Paul de Man*. Trans. Cecile Lindsay, Jonathan Culler and Eduardo Cadava. New York: Columbia University Press.

——. 1992. Afterw.rds or, at least, less than a letter about a letter less. Trans. Geoffrey Bennington, in Nicholas Royle (ed.), *Afterwords* (Tampere English Studies 1), pp.197–203. Tampere: University of Tampere.

——. 1998. *Monolingualism of the Other, or The Prothesis of Origin*. Trans. Patrick Mensah. Stanford: Stanford University Press.

—— and Geoffrey Bennington. 1993. *Jacques Derrida*. Trans. G. Bennington. London and Chicago: University of Chicago Press.

Readings, Bill. 1989. The deconstruction of politics. In Lindsay Waters and Wlad Godzich (eds.), *Reading de Man Reading*, pp.223–43. Minneapolis: University of Minnesota Press.

7

On Dialectology

ROBERT PENHALLURICK

I. The object of dialectology

It can be argued that, compared with its early years, present-day dialectology shows a diversity of approaches and interests. But this diversity happens within limits which have been constant since the days of Alexander J. Ellis (1814–90). Ellis described the business of dialectology in his presidential addresses of 1872–4 to the Philological Society. That business would be collection without prejudice:

> [W]ord-collectors are not generally philosophic linguists. Their business is to hand over the materials in a trustworthy form, unadulterated with superficial and superfluous additions, containing what is wanted and *no more*, to those who *are* philosophic linguists. (Ellis 1874, 450; italics in the original)

According to the limits described by Ellis, dialectology is in the business of *delivery*. Like a mail company, dialectology delivers goods safely and securely from a source to a destination. The goods are not to be tampered with en route, in carriage.

Details of the emergence of dialectology as a scholarly discipline in Europe from the latter part of the nineteenth century onwards, of its considerable debt to comparative philology, of its early and prolonged enthusiasm for the production of atlases, glossaries and dictionaries, of its difficulties with and accommodations of structuralism and late twentieth-century sociolinguistics can be found elsewhere, for example in differing measures in the introductory books by Petyt (1980), Francis (1983) and Chambers and Trudgill

(1998). This history, and its telling in these introductory texts, is also discussed by Graham Shorrocks in the present volume. Suffice it to say at this point that dialectology's history as a recognizable discipline is marked by influences and buffetings from other branches of academic study, and that as a result it has evolved and diversified. Also it is now more difficult than ever to identify a clear boundary separating dialectology and sociolinguistics. In this essay, I am not going to try to – though Clive Upton does in his contribution to the present volume. My concern here is with a fundamental quality of dialectology which I believe has been constant since the time of A. J. Ellis, and which Ellis articulated so explicitly. It is, briefly, the view that dialectologists are neutral observers and collectors of language, data collectors, but not 'philosophers' or 'theorists' – a position which Jeni Williams interrogates with regard to the study of dialect in literature, in her essay in this volume. The same broad characteristic underpins sociolinguistics. The present essay examines some paradoxes that issue from this characteristic.

Whilst the word *dialect* appeared in English in the sixteenth century, *dialectology* arrived, according to the *Oxford English Dictionary*, in 1879. In fact, the term was used by Ellis in 1874, in his third address to the Philological Society as its president. That and his first and second addresses in 1872 and 1873 amount to something of a manifesto for dialectology in England and beyond, laying out, for example, a clear historical interest ('we cannot at all properly understand varied Early English – which consists solely of dialects – without understanding the varied English of to-day', 1873b, 248) and a keen sense of urgency ('Intercommunication is drawing a wet sponge over the living records of our nascent tongue', 1873b, 248 – cf. Shorrocks again in the present volume). But it is Ellis's comments on word-collectors and their business that are most prescient.

Since A. J. Ellis there has been little disagreement amongst dialectologists over the destination of the goods that they collect and deliver. There are three groups of receivers or addressees: dialectologists themselves, the prime group; other language scholars or, in the words of Joseph Wright, 'the present and all future generations of students of our mother-tongue' (1898, v); and 'the general reader' (Wright 1898, v). As for Ellis's deliverees, the 'philosophic linguists', maybe they are there in the second group. Of greater interest than the destination are the source and the process of delivery. The source or the object of dialectology might be encapsulated in the label *everyday living speech*. A. J. Ellis wished for attention to be focused on 'existing forms of speech', especially 'on those [forms] not possessing a literature, and the peasant dialects of those which do possess one, as the real fermenting mass whence language grows' (1873a, 32–3). In the mid-twentieth century, Harold Orton wanted to describe 'genuine vernacular' (1962, 15), and his collaborator Eugen Dieth wanted each fieldworker of their Survey of English Dialects to be 'capable of recognizing an adulterated form and keen to probe his source for the real thing' (Orton and Dieth 1951, 69). Similarly, in sociolinguistics, scholars aim to describe 'the language of real people as they speak it in the course of their everyday lives' (Trudgill 1994, ix), or to elicit 'a speech style as close as possible to a speaker's spontaneous, everyday speech' (Milroy 1987, 57). Ellis was eager to shift the emphasis of language research away from the study of written texts to the study of speech, away from the 'dead masks' of the letters of the alphabet to the 'living faces' of speech-sounds (1874, 449). Orton and Dieth, in their history-orientated Survey of English Dialects, wanted to collect from the most conservative stratum of everyday living speech. The sociolinguist Lesley Milroy concedes that, 'like many other metalinguistic concepts, the concept of the vernacular is not particularly well-defined' (1987, 59), but adds that 'this need not be a problem if we treat a speaker's or a community's vernacular as an abstract object' (1987, 59). Her aim is to debunk the notion of 'a completely spontaneous and natural speech style' (1987, 60) and reconfigure it as a structural abstraction, a comparative rather than an absolute object. Although her reconfiguration is expressed according to the taxonomy of structural sociolinguistics, the object she speaks of is not fundamentally different from A. J. Ellis's living, teeming language and Harold Orton's 'genuine vernacular', both of which are also comparative entities. And it is as a comparative entity that *everyday living speech* becomes paradoxical. The concept encompasses vitality and diversity, but also ordinariness and straightforwardness. *Everyday living speech* is consequently seen to be unencumbered by the acknowledged complexities of other forms of language that are placed in contrast to it, literature being a conspicuous example. As such it becomes amenable to collection. Indeed, it is only as such an unproblematic object that it can become collectable. The concept, which is also the object of dialectology, is thus transformed into *data*, in the process losing that difficult and unmanageable quality which defined it originally – vitality.

For A. J. Ellis in 1874, the top priority with regard to data was the pronunciation of living speech: 'It is only by serious study of phonology that we can raise dialectology to the rank of philology. When we know the words, then we can go really to work on meaning, descent, idiom, grammar, thought' (1874, 449). The last item in his list, and its position as last, is significant. In order to clarify, let me recount a mundane conversation.

I was visiting an old friend. He was preparing the evening meal. On entering the kitchen, I said, 'Mushrooms'. He replied, 'Yes, mushrooms. I am preparing the mushrooms. I have been preparing the mushrooms for some time and you had better not renege now on your earlier commitment otherwise I might be rather annoyed.' After a pause, I replied, 'All I said was "mushrooms".' After another pause, my friend said, 'Ah yes, well done, very good.'

There was no one else present. Had there been, they might have been unable to comprehend the full meaning of the exchange. They might not have recognized the 'winding-up' that was going on. The exchange cannot be fully explicated without reference to an exchange which the two of us had had earlier that day, which itself referred back to a conversation the day before, which itself referred back to events and exchanges some years before. The winding-up depended on a shared knowledge of previous events and of our interactions down the years. One could even say that an explication of the exchange above requires study of the psychology of our friendship, and in the absence of that its full meaning remains a little obscure. In other words, it demands that concepts such as emotion, memory and thought be considered.

A small number of further observations can be made here in connection with the example above. Firstly, given its peculiar circumstances, the exchange could be said to be untypical of everyday living speech. Nevertheless, its peculiar circumstances might be taken to be exemplary. Once one acknowledges the relevance of concepts like memory and thought, then it becomes more difficult to describe any linguistic exchange as typical. One could only say that an exchange typically will have peculiar circumstances. Secondly, it is evident that the full meaning of the exchange above cannot be deduced from the sum of its sounds, or from the sum of its words, or its grammatical constructions. Such observations as these are not original, even in linguistics. But clearly, for a discipline like dialectology, whose mission is to set about collecting and delivering large amounts of 'materials', explications and even 'materials' of the type sketched out above are impractical. Such a discipline needs to reduce the tangled, teeming complexities of mundane discourse to manageable, deliverable proportions. It needs to postpone indefinitely consideration of 'thought', to regard meaning as confinable to a single time and place, and to diminish further the dynamics of verbal interaction by treating speech as reducible to brief segments. It is not that these things are required so that explication can be avoided; they are required in order to render everyday living speech deliverable. And that itself is a form of explication.

In this way are the original aims of dialectology turned back on themselves. The 'handing over of materials' envisaged by A. J. Ellis was never going to be *delivery* plain and simple, for it would entail *presentation*. The materials would have to be organized, and this would entail, at the very least, implicit explication at the point of delivery. Explication at the point of delivery has never been avoided in dialectology, it has merely been constrained by and defined by *deliverability*. Explication and deliverability are not in conflict. In dialectology, it is delivery which is compromised by deliverability. That is, deliverability leads to a view of language, an explication of language, that reduces living language to data. This explication, as well as arising out of deliverability, is a prerequisite of deliverability. This explication is not supposed to happen, for the purpose of dialectology is to provide the materials that will enable explication. But the purpose demands an explication of language before it can be collected. Before collection has begun the materials of dialectology have been 'pre-explicated'. Dialectologists turn out to be philosphic linguists after all!

This inevitably has consequences for those engaged in the practice of dialectology, who find a mismatch between the pre-explicated *everyday living speech* that has become the object of dialectology and the language that they encounter during their collecting expeditions. A. J. Ellis argued that the study of language had to be focused on the 'long and troublesome living examination of living speech', not on ancient manuscripts – on the 'relations of life' and not on the 'bones of the dead' (1873a, 22).

> Laborious as it may be to pore over manuscripts . . . the labour is as
> nothing compared to the patient watching of habits, registering of
> usages, slow acquirement of uncongenial thought, accurate apprecia-
> tion of living changing sounds, in thousands of thousands of
> instances, on which we must base our real science of language. (Ellis
> 1873a, 22)

The mismatch is summed up in this passage, which pitches the
defiant vitality of language against the requirements of 'real science',
reducing language to the collectable, measurable 'thousands of
thousands of instances'. For the 'mass of drilled soldiery' (Ellis 1874,
448), the fieldworking dialectologists seeking 'instances', the 'field'
throws up one quandary after another: where to go to find the
instances, whom to get them from, how many 'informants', how to
talk to them, whether to talk to them, whether to question them,
how to record them, how to transcribe, how much to transcribe, and
so on. Every problem has its pragmatic solution, but giving rise to
each quandary is the mismatch between the constructed object of
dialectology and the wilfulness of living language.

The object of dialectology is constructed, formed, in a sense
completed, by dialectology before dialectology begins. In a sense,
dialectology delivers the completed object before dialectology
begins. The practice of dialectology merely falteringly sustains the
object. The 'object' resists objectification. (As Donna Haraway puts
it: 'The codes of the world are not still, waiting only to be read'
(1991, 198)). A subject is also constructed: the collector, the
dialectologist who delivers the materials. The subject is constructed
as passive, divided from and external to the object, an observer – an
untenable position. The object of dialectology is always on the brink
of collapsing into the subject of dialectology, for both object and
subject are restlessly active. Despite itself, dialectology is a kind
of conversation.

II.   The subject of dialectology

Dialectology in the British Isles is finished, in that its project is over
and done with. The aim of dialectology in Britain – and elsewhere
also – has been to collect and publish data. There have been

national dialect surveys in all of the countries of the British Isles, and many regional and local surveys led up to and followed on from the national surveys. The urgent work for which A. J. Ellis called has been done.

On the other hand, the dialectological project can never be finished. The dialectology of English is a worldwide concern, but even the dialectology of English in Britain has no end as long as the English language is used in Britain. There will always be data for dialectologists to amass, and collection to be done urgently. The dialectology inaugurated by A. J. Ellis can run endlessly.

The legacy of this project which is already finished and which can never be finished is data. The main aim or end of dialectology is data, an endless end. There will never be a moment when the dialectologist can say, 'Now we have collected all the data that there is to collect.' The data still have to be delivered, and they are delivered via a variety of methodologies and formats, but Ellis's maxim about delivering 'the materials in a trustworthy form' continues to resonate because it ensures the neutrality of the dialectologist's practice. It allows the dialectologist to assume that dialectology is a practice without theory, which is a highly theorized position.

The practice of dialectology entails another paradox, one given a name by the sociolinguist William Labov: the *observer's paradox*.

> Granted the ability to pass beyond ideological, technical, and social constraints, and the recognition of the disjunctions between norms and behavior, there remains a crucial methodological paradox in the study of everyday language . . .
>
> THE OBSERVER'S PARADOX: *To obtain the data most important for linguistic theory, we have to observe how people speak when they are not being observed.* (Labov 1972, 112–13)

One could make the pedantic point that it is quite usual for people to be observed when they speak, and perhaps less usual for them to be unobserved, but of course Labov is referring to the scholarly observer. Less finicky is the proposal that such an observer cannot exist. This is not to suggest that scholars do not exist. It is rather to complement Nicholas Royle's suggestion in the present volume that the dialectologist does not exist, that is, that there cannot be a practitioner who is external to the practice in which he or she engages. Labov is concerned with the puzzle facing the language researcher who wishes to observe (and collect), in the 'field', 'natural speech' (Labov 1972, 108). One way to formulate the puzzle is Labov's: the presence of the 'observer' determines that the speech event will not be 'natural'. Another way is to propose that if the 'observer' is present then he or she will no longer be an 'observer' but a participant, subject to the speech event. In this way the paradox of the observer is that there can be no observer.

This line can be taken further. The 'constraints' that Labov mentions are those that 'prevent linguists from utilizing the wealth of linguistic data with which they are surrounded', that is, 'the barriers against interaction with strangers in one's own culture' (1972, 110). For Labov there are methodological adjustments which can circumvent these barriers. In using the word 'constraints', Labov is not, apparently, referring to the impossibility of *any* procedure untrammelled by ideology or belief or cultural context. There can be no party, no 'observer', who is external to *such* 'constraints'.

Similarly, there can be no Labovian 'observer' of language. As Roland Barthes put it, 'Unfortunately, human language has no exterior: there is no exit' (1982, 461). There cannot be a practitioner who is not party to language, a circumstance acknowledged and compounded by the thriving metalanguages of linguistics. Everyone is subject to dialect.

Not all of the essays in the present collection have discussed the dialectologist as a construct, but all have attempted a fundamental reassessment of the role of the dialectologist. All too have, from quite different perspectives, presented innovative views on the nature of dialect.

The *OED* says that *dialect* can be traced back to Greek διάλεκτοζ, meaning 'discourse, conversation, way of speaking', as well as 'language of a country or district', from διαλέγεσθαι 'to discourse, converse', from δια- 'through, across' +λέγειν 'to speak'. The object of dialectology (manageable everyday living speech) and the subject of dialectology (the neutral observer) are constructs essential to the discipline and its achievements, but they *are* constructs, and if constructs could be said to creak, or to be in danger of falling apart at the seams, then these constructs do so perpetually. Dialect is discourse, speaking through and across, alive and teeming, and the dialectologist, like everyone, is subject to dialect. Despite everything, the fate of the dialectologist is to be an active participant in conversation.

Works cited

Barthes, Roland. 1982. Inaugural lecture, Collège de France. Trans. Richard Howard. In Susan Sontag (ed.), *A Barthes Reader*, pp.457–78. London: Vintage, 1993 (originally published in English in 1982; lecture delivered 7 January 1977).

Chambers, J. K. and Peter Trudgill. 1998. *Dialectology*. 2nd edition. Cambridge: Cambridge University Press.

Ellis, Alexander J. 1873a. First annual address of the president to the Philological Society, delivered at the anniversary meeting, Friday, 17th May, 1872. *Transactions of the Philological Society* (1873–4), I, 1–34.

——. 1873b. Second annual address of the president to the Philological Society, delivered at the anniversary meeting, Friday, 16th May, 1873: report by the president on the formation of an English Dialect Society. *Transactions of the Philological Society* (1873–4), II, 247–8.

——. 1874. Third annual address of the president to the Philological Society, delivered at the anniversary meeting, Friday, 15th May, 1874: the president on English dialectology. *Transactions of the Philological Society* (1873–4), III, 447–51.

Francis, W. N. 1983. *Dialectology: An Introduction*. London: Longman.

Haraway, Donna J. 1991. *Simians, Cyborgs, and Women: The Reinvention of Nature*. London: Free Association Books.

Labov, William. 1972. Some principles of linguistic methodology. *Language in Society*, 1 (1972), 97–120.

Milroy, Lesley. 1987. *Observing and Analysing Natural Language: A Critical Account of Sociolinguistic Method*. Oxford: Basil Blackwell.

Orton, Harold. 1962. *Survey of English Dialects (A): Introduction*. Leeds: E. J. Arnold.

—— and Eugen Dieth. 1951. The new survey of dialectal English. In C. L. Wrenn and G. Bullough (eds.), *English Studies To-day*, pp.63–73. Oxford: Oxford University Press, 1951. (Part I of this essay is by Orton, part II by Dieth.)

Petyt, K. M. 1980. *The Study of Dialect: An Introduction to Dialectology*. London: André Deutsch.

Trudgill, Peter. 1994. Editor's Preface. In William Labov, *Principles of Linguistic Change. Volume I: Internal Factors*, p.ix. Oxford: Blackwell, 1994.

Wright, Joseph (ed.). 1898. *The English Dialect Dictionary*. Volume I. Oxford: Frowde.

Index of Names and Topics

(For full lists of all authors referred to in this volume see the bibliographies at the ends of chapters.)